AF213708

Springer Studies in Alternative Economics

This book series offers an outlet for cutting-edge research in alternative, heterodox and pluralist economics. It features scholarly studies on various schools of thought beyond the neo-classical orthodoxy, including Austrian, Post Keynesian, Sraffian, Marxian, Georgist, Institutional-evolutionary, as well as feminist, radical, social, green, and ecological economics. It aims to promote pluralism of economic ideas, methodological approaches, and topics.

The series also welcomes works that seek to develop alternative visions of the economy, economic structures and new approaches that aim to serve society, for example by embedding the economy within the ecosystem, or to enrich economic thought by advancing diversity, gender, race, and social equality. All titles in this series are peer-reviewed.

Laszlo Zsolnai

Planet Positive Economy

Ethical, Spiritual, and Methodological Foundations

Springer

Laszlo Zsolnai
Business Ethics Center
Corvinus University of Budapest
Budapest, Hungary

Blackfriars Hall
University of Oxford
Oxford, UK

ISSN 2731-5908 ISSN 2731-5916 (electronic)
Springer Studies in Alternative Economics
ISBN 978-3-032-21130-9 ISBN 978-3-032-21131-6 (eBook)
https://doi.org/10.1007/978-3-032-21131-6

© The Editor(s) (if applicable) and The Author(s), under exclusive license to Springer Nature Switzerland AG 2026

This work is subject to copyright. All rights are solely and exclusively licensed by the Publisher, whether the whole or part of the material is concerned, specifically the rights of translation, reprinting, reuse of illustrations, recitation, broadcasting, reproduction on microfilms or in any other physical way, and transmission or information storage and retrieval, electronic adaptation, computer software, or by similar or dissimilar methodology now known or hereafter developed.
The use of general descriptive names, registered names, trademarks, service marks, etc. in this publication does not imply, even in the absence of a specific statement, that such names are exempt from the relevant protective laws and regulations and therefore free for general use.
The publisher, the authors and the editors are safe to assume that the advice and information in this book are believed to be true and accurate at the date of publication. Neither the publisher nor the authors or the editors give a warranty, expressed or implied, with respect to the material contained herein or for any errors or omissions that may have been made. The publisher remains neutral with regard to jurisdictional claims in published maps and institutional affiliations.

This Springer imprint is published by the registered company Springer Nature Switzerland AG.
The registered company address is: Gewerbestrasse 11, 6330 Cham, Switzerland

If disposing of this product, please recycle the paper.

Preface

Our planet is in danger. The climate system is rapidly approaching a tipping point beyond which there will be no return to the previous climatic conditions under which humanity developed over millennia. Worsening environmental and societal trends, including biodiversity loss, ecosystem collapses, mass migration, social unrest, international wars, and the dangerous applications of AI, pose an existential risk to humanity's survival.

In response to the so-called "polycrisis" of our age, authoritarian, nationalist, and fundamentalist governments have come to power (e.g., in China, India, and the USA). President Trump has withdrawn the United States from the Paris Climate Treaty, and the EU is scaling back its ambitious Green Deal program.

Decades ago, American eco-philosopher Thomas Berry, C.P., famously said: "From here on, the primary judgement of all human institutions, professions, programs and activities will be determined by the extent to which they inhibit, ignore or foster a mutually enhancing human-Earth relationship."

The papers collected in this book aim to inspire and help people, communities, and organizations develop actions, systems, and policies that foster the kind of changes necessary for the long-term flourishing of humanity and the Earth. Planet positive changes are not only beneficial for humans and non-human beings but also valuable in their own right, and may have cosmic significance.

December 31, 2025 — Laszlo Zsolnai

Preface

Acknowledgments The author would like to thank *Taylor & Francis*, *The Way* (Oxford), and *Springer* for permission to reproduce some of his previously published papers in this book. Also, the author expresses his gratitude to *Paul Shrivastava* (Pennsylvania State University & The Club of Rome), *Ora Setter* (formerly Tel Aviv University), and *Gabor Kovacs*, *Andras Ocsai*, *Kalman Kelemen*, and *Zoltan Valcsicsak* (Corvinus University of Budapest) for their permission to include papers in this book that were jointly written with them.

In an earlier stage of this book's development, the author received helpful comments and suggestions from *Clair Brown* (University of California, Berkeley), *Sanjoy Mukherjee* (Indian Institute of Management – Shillong), and *Fumiko Kasuga* (Future Earth Global Hub, Tokyo). Additionally, the author is grateful for the encouragement and assistance he has received from *Lorraine Klimovich*, Senior Editor at Springer.

Competing Interests The author has no competing interests to declare that are relevant to the content of this manuscript.

Acknowledgments.

Contents

List of Figures

List of Tables

Chapter 1
Introduction

1.1 What is Planet Positivity?

Our era, in which humanity is altering the biogeochemistry of the planet itself, destabilizing the climate, and influencing coevolution at the planetary level, is rightly called "the Anthropocene" (Crutzen, 2002; Steffen et al., 2011). The Anthropocene appears to be a regrettable exit from the Holocene, the relatively placid period of the past 10,000 years, characterized by climate stability during which "civilization" emerged (Brown, 2015).

1.2 The Reality of the Anthropocene

Important indicators show that the state of the Earth (the sum of our planet's interacting physical, chemical, biological, and human processes) has drastically worsened over the last 75 years. This process has been referred to as "The Great Acceleration" (IGBP, 2015). Research documents that socioeconomic trends (such as population, real GDP, foreign direct investment, urban population, primary energy use, fertilizer consumption, water use, paper production, transportation, telecommunications, and international tourism) have led to a deterioration in numerous Earth Systems (such as carbon dioxide, nitrous oxide, methane, surface temperature, ocean acidification, marine fish capture, tropical forest loss, domesticated land, and terrestrial biosphere) since the 1950s.

Planetary boundaries define the safe operating space for humanity on Earth. They include climate change, changes in biosphere integrity (involving biodiversity loss and species extinction), stratospheric ozone depletion, ocean acidification, biogeochemical cycles (such as phosphorus and nitrogen), land-system change (for example, deforestation), and freshwater use. Current research on planetary

© The Author(s), under exclusive license to Springer Nature Switzerland AG 2026

L. Zsolnai, *Planet Positive Economy*, Springer Studies in Alternative Economics,
https://doi.org/10.1007/978-3-032-21131-6_1

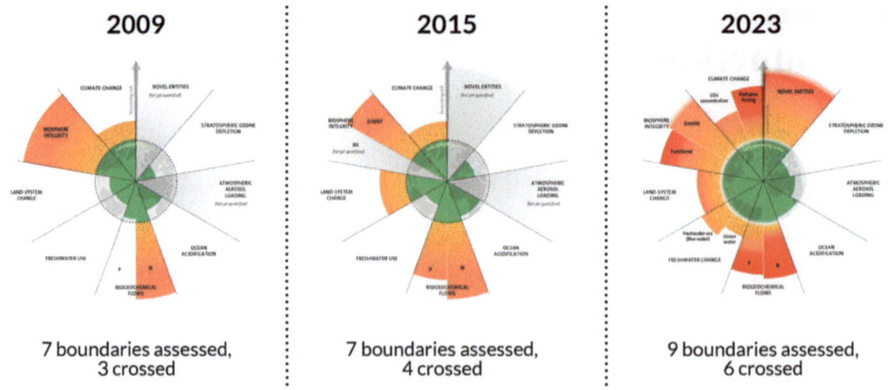

Fig. 1.1 Planetary boundaries in 2009–2023. *Source* Azote for Stockholm Resilience Centre, based on analysis Sakschewski et al. (2025)

boundaries indicates that humanity is transgressing critical biophysical limits, beyond which the environment may no longer be able to self-regulate (Stockholm Resilience Centre, 2024) (Fig. 1.1).

The Anthropocene has mainly been caused by the cumulative effects of business activities over the last 75 years. This dramatic deterioration of the capacity of Earth to support life is mainly due to current patterns of production and consumption. Business activities have come to dominate all spheres of life almost everywhere on the planet. In disregarding the carrying capacity of ecosystems, business activities place huge burdens on present and future life forms (human and nonhuman alike).

In summary, we can say that the Anthropocene era presents a set of interrelated, messy, and "wicked" problems that have been referred to as a "polycrisis" (Albert, 2024). These challenges are so profound that they pose an existential threat to humanity and could lead to the collapse of human civilization. The continued existence and survival of the human species on Earth have now become uncertain (Stanford, 2024).

1.3 The Concept of Planet Positivity

The concept of "planet positivity" was introduced and popularized in the "Strong Sustainability by Design" report by the Institute of Electrical and Electronics Engineers (IEEE) Standards Association in the USA (IEEE Planet Positive Initiative, 2024). Several hundred thought leaders from academia, industry, civil society, policy, and government worked on this. I had the opportunity to contribute directly to this report and have worked on building consensus about the critical issues concerning the fate of our planet.

Planet positivity can be understood as actions and policies that make positive contributions to the long-term flourishing of the planet by conjointly serving the well-being of people and the regeneration or preservation of nature.

"Planet positivity" is a fractal-like concept, meaning it can be interpreted at different levels of the Humanity-Earth nexus, from individuals and communities to industries, countries, regions, and the world as a whole.

Also, the concept can be applied to a variety of economic players including (1) business organizations (corporations, unincorporated businesses, social enterprises), (2) financial institutions (central banks, commercial banks, investment funds, pension funds, insurance companies), (3) public service organizations (education, healthcare, utilities), (4) households (the super-rich, upper-class, middle-class, poor, and marginalized), (5) local communities (cities, towns, villages), (6) virtual communities (Facebook, LinkedIn, X), (7) political bodies (parliaments, central and local governments, international organizations), (8) legal institutions (courts of justice, law firms), (9) cultural institutions (churches, universities, R&D organizations, art institutions), (10) media (print, online, and audio-visual), (11) civil society organizations (environmental, human rights, cultural), (12) professional associations (chambers of commerce, etc.), (13) trade unions, (14) clusters, and even (15) robots (algorithms and physical) (Zsolnai, 2018). These actors differ ontologically (i.e., their motivations, cognitive capacities, and moral capabilities vary), but all contribute to the fate of the planet positively or negatively.

The ultimate goal of a *planet-positive economy* is not to foster material economic growth, but to *provide livelihoods for people in a just and sustainable manner*. This cannot be achieved if economic actors are driven by a materialistic value orientation.

A materialistic value orientation involves prioritizing material values, such as money, possessions, sensual pleasure, and social recognition, and the self-centered pursuit of these values. A materialistic value orientation can lead to antisocial and environmentally degrading behavior (Kasser, 2011).

A planet-positive economy can only be created by economic actors who follow a spiritual value orientation. This approach prioritizes nonmaterialistic values such as love, frugality, compassion, and humility, and pursues these objectives in caring and peaceful ways (Bouckaert & Zsolnai, 2012).

1.4 Issues and Themes

This book's chapters investigate the ethical, spiritual, and methodological foundations of planet positivity in relation to the economy.

The chapter "Spirituality and Economics" shows that in its current form, economics is a materialist and reductionist science. It critiques the core assumptions of mainstream economics and demonstrates that they lead to an economy that is detrimental to people and renders the planet unsustainable. The chapter argues for a spiritual turn in economics that cultivates the best (and not the worst) of human nature. The emerging postmaterialist economics acknowledges both the material and the nonmaterial aspects of human existence. The chapter presents directions for the development of postmaterialist economics and concludes that by helping to create ecological and human economic practices and policies, postmaterialist economics can support the flourishing of life on Earth.

The chapter entitled "The Economics of Pope Francis" analyses Pope Francis' economic views. It shows the relationship of St. Francis of Assisi, who inspired Pope Francis, to the economy and then explores, among other documents, the main economic messages contained in the papal encyclical *Laudato si'*. Finally, the chapter presents Pope Francis's "The Economy of Francesco" initiative and discusses further opportunities for development.

The chapter on "Buddhist Economics" examines Buddhist economics as an economic conception that is radically different from Western economics. Buddhist economics presupposes that the world is interdependent, that people are altruistic, and that happiness comes from caring for others and the Earth. Buddhism suggests operational guiding principles for economic action, as follows: (1) reducing the suffering of sentient beings, (2) minimizing desires and attachment, (3) genuine care for others, (4) nonviolence (*ahimsa*), and (5) generosity (giving without expecting anything in return). The chapter argues that although Buddhism is culturally rooted in the east, it represents a viable alternative approach for western economic systems.

The chapter "Lessons from Hindu Spirituality" shows how Hindu spirituality can be used in contemporary management. It presents S. K. Chakraborty's attempts to integrate Hindu spirituality into management, drawing on insights from Vedanta philosophy and the works of modern proponents such as Rabindranath Tagore, Swami Vivekananda, Mahatma Gandhi, and Sri Aurobindo. Finally, the case of Aravind Eye Care System is discussed to illustrate how Hindu spirituality can catalyze alternative ways of thinking and organizing for a safe and sane future.

The chapter "Indigenous Worldviews" highlights that the panpsychism and holism associated with indigenous worldviews represent an alternative to materialism and reductionism of modern economics and business. It emphasizes that indigenous worldviews suggest that economic activities should be organized in community-based, substantive ways, respecting the limits of the natural environment. The chapter presents Seventh Generation and Jokkmokk's Market as working models inspired by indigenous worldviews.

The chapter on "Misfunctions and Blind Spots of Mainstream Businesses" presents the vicious circle of corporate functioning where different elements intensify and aggravate each other, leading inexorably to a worsening of the situation. Today, financial wealth creation is the primary goal of corporations and other mainstream businesses. This leads to appropriating values from common natural and societal resources without paying the price for it, and to externalizing most of the costs upon society, nature, and future generations. By their functioning, corporations create environmental and social ils and develop some blind spots to avoid seeing and recognizing the environmental and social harms caused by their activities. As a response to the perceived environmental and social ills, society demands more economic growth. The circle is closed by financial markets, which put huge pressure on mainstream business organizations for growth and money.

The chapter entitled "The Virtuous Circle of Corporate Functioning" reviews different directions of corporate reform including the purpose model, B-corporations, the net-positive initiative, the conscious capitalism movement, impact investing, and long-term stock exchange, and new measures of business performance. Then, an integrated vision for corporate well-functioning is presented. In this model, the elements form a virtuous circle in which one desirable occurrence leads to another, which may result in a continuous process of improvement. A well-functioning business has a purpose related to sustainable value creation, which involves the company being managed for all the stakeholders, not only for a special group (e.g., the shareholders or the owners). Well-functioning businesses use only their "fair share" from the common resources and internalize the social and environmental costs of their functioning. They develop multiple "win & win" solutions which are simultaneously beneficial for people, for nature, for future generations, and for the companies themselves. They make efforts to change the materialistic mindset of their customers and other stakeholders by prioritizing nonmaterialist values and goals. The circle is closed by investors and financial institutions with a long-term perspective who have an active interest in promoting the integral development of people and the planet.

The chapter "Living with Non-Materialistic Values" discusses the negative consequences of the materialistic value orientation that dominates today's economic and business practices. It argues that to create a planet-positive economy, a spiritual value orientation should be adopted that prioritizes nonmaterial values over material ones. Finally, the so-called "Pascal's Wager" is revisited to show the reasonableness of opting for spirituality over materialism.

The chapter "Self-Interest or Higher Purpose?" uses the case of modern agribusiness as an experimentum crucis (a decisive experiment) to illustrate the devastating effects of the self-interest-based functioning of modern mainstream corporations. As an alternative, the case of slow food is presented. The chapter also discusses the so-called "crowding effect" in the economic context. Under specific conditions, market coordination may "crowd out" ethical motivation because the frame of reference shifts from moral considerations to cost-benefit calculations. Fortunately, there are also conditions under which ethical motivation may "crowd in" market coordination (when cost-benefit calculations strengthen moral considerations). The central proposition of the chapter is that the self-interest-based doctrine of modern economics should be changed. To serve public happiness and ecological sustainability, intrinsic (ethical) motivation should be prioritized over extrinsic (financial) motivation. The civil economy tradition can help us accomplish this shift. The chapter concludes that we need to develop economic arrangements that combine ethics and the market in a mutually supportive way. However, acting for the "higher purpose" should always take precedence over self-interest in business and economic life, if we wish to survive and flourish in the Anthropocene era.

The chapter on "Value Creation in the Anthropocene" discusses the grand challenges of the Anthropocene era. It introduces the concept of "sustainable value creation" understood as products, processes, organizations, and actions that satisfy real human needs and make positive impacts on nature, society, and future generations. The chapter also presents the most important features of sustainable value creation, including (1) promoting frugality, (2) acknowledging the intrinsic value of nature, (3) producing negative emissions, and (4) developing ecologically regenerative projects.

The chapter "Wellbeing Policies for Countries and Cities" begins with the observation that most countries and cities today follow policies that prioritize competitiveness, economic growth, and material wealth creation, which often produce considerable "ills" in the Anthropocene. The chapter presents some of the leading alternative approaches that countries and cities have developed to create wellbeing in a broad socio-ecological context. These include the Gross National Happiness Framework in Bhutan, Costa Rica's National Decarbonization Plan, the Wellbeing Budget of New Zealand, and the "Doughnut Economy" model of Amsterdam. These initiatives abandon the idea of GDP-centered economic growth, instead directly targeting increased human well-being and promoting ecological regeneration.

The chapter "Identifying and Solving the Right Problems" argues that it is a serious failure of business and management to solve the wrong problems. Erroneous problem formulations can lead to disastrous consequences for the well-being of stakeholders. To avoid substantive failures in problem solving, business and management practitioners should reconsider the basic assumptions concerning the system in which they operate and include the views of as many stakeholders as possible. Appropriate problem solutions should address all the important dimensions of the problems in question (the scientific-technical, the interpersonal-social, the systemic-ecological, and the existential-spiritual) and aim for optimal balance among them. The job of responsible business and management is to identify the right problems and produce solutions that are substantively adequate and ethically acceptable.

The chapter "Methodology for Systems Change" presents the different levels of intervention in a system (parameters, feedback, design, and purpose). Then it classifies possible strategies for interacting with organizations ("non-cooperation," "reforming," "cooperation," and "creating") to avoid increasing social and environmental ill-being and/or creating socio-ecological well-being.

The chapter entitled "Ethics Needs Spirituality" discusses the relationship between ethics and spirituality. It shows that business ethics lacks a deeper existential-spiritual foundation, which leads to the inadequate and ineffective functioning of today's mainstream business and management. The chapter advocates for the application of spirituality-based ethics in business and management.

The chapter "Care, and Its Relevance to Today's Economy" emphasizes that care is a central aspect of human existence. What we care about and who we care for largely determine our being and acting. The "imperative of responsibility" suggests that nature, human beings, and future generations should be considered as the primary subjects of care in business and management. Economic actors must develop practices that incorporate genuine interest in and caring for the existence and well-being of these primordial "stakeholders." We care for other beings because of our deeply felt humanity, but in many cases, caring for others also serves our best interests. However, the primary motive underlying genuine care should not be self-interest, but our responsibility for the existence and well-being of others.

The chapter titled "Selflessly Helping Others and the Planet" presents a self-interview with the author of this book. It reveals the author's spiritual development and advances an ethical position that highlights the importance of altruistic acts directed at human and nonhuman beings.

Overall, the book investigates the possible conditions of a planet's positive economy. Based on the arguments presented herein, two theorems are generated. One concerns the "impossibility condition" of a planet's positive economy, and the other the "possibility condition."

The Impossibility Theorem of Planet Positive Economy:

A planet-positive economy cannot be achieved by economic agents who pursue a materialistic value orientation.

The Possibility Theorem of Planet Positive Economy:

Economic agents who pursue a spiritual value orientation have a chance to create a planet positive economy.

If these theorems are true, the behavior of economic players and their working models should undergo a radical transformation. Our survival and flourishing depend on the success of this transformation.

References

Albert, M. J. (2024). *Navigating the polycrisis: Mapping the futures of capitalism and the Earth.* MIT Press.

Bouckaert, L., & Zsolnai, L. (2012). Spirituality and business: An interdisciplinary overview. *Society and Economy, 34*(3), 489–514.

Brown, P. G. (2015). Ethics for economics in the anthropocene. In P. G. Brown & P. Timmerman (Eds.), *Ecological economics for the Anthropocene. An emerging paradigm* (pp. 66–88). Columbia University Press.

Crutzen, P. J. (2002). Geology of mankind. *Nature, 415*(3).

IEEE Planet Positive Initiative. (2024). *Strong sustainability by design: Prioritizing ecosystem and human flourishing with technology-based solutions.* IEEE. https://sagroups.ieee.org/planetpositive2030/our-work/. Accessed February 17, 2025.

IGBP. (2015). *The great acceleration.* https://www.stockholmresilience.org/research/research-news/2015-01-15-new-planetary-dashboard-shows-increasing-human-impact.html. Accessed October 3, 2024.

Kasser, T. (2011). Materialistic value-orientation. In L. Bouckaert & L. Zsolnai (Eds.), *The Palgrave handbook of spirituality and business* (pp. 204–211). Palgrave-Macmillan.

Sakschewski, B., Caesar, L., Andersen, L. S., Bechthold, M., Bergfeld, L., Beusen, A., Billing, M., Bodirsky, B. L., Botsyun, S., Dennis, D. P., Donges, J. F., Dou, X., Eriksson, A., Fetzer, I., Gerten, D., Häyhä, T., Hebden, S., Heckmann, T., Heilemann, A., … Rockström, J. (2025). *Planetary health check 2025: A scientific assessment of the state of the planet*. Potsdam Institute for Climate Impact Research. https://doi.org/10.48485/pik.2025.017.

Stanford. (2024). *Existential risks initiative*. https://seri.stanford.edu/. Accessed October 3, 2024.

Steffen, W., Persson, A., Deutsch, L., Zalasiewicz, J., Williams, M., Richardson, K., Crumley, C., Crutzen, P., Folke, C., Gordon, L., Molina, M., Ramanathan, V., Rockström, J., Scheffer, M., Schellnhuber, H. J., & Svedin, U. (2011). The Anthropocene: From global change to planetary stewardship. *Ambio*, *40*(7), 739–761.

Stockholm Resilience Centre. (2024). *Planetary Boundaries 2009–2023*. https://www.stockholmresilience.org/research/planetary-boundaries.html. Accessed June 1, 2024.

Zsolnai, L. (2018). Economic actors and the ultimate goal of the economy. In P. Rona & L. Zsolnai (Eds.), *Economic objects and the objects of economics* (pp. 151–159). Springer.

Part I
The Spiritual Perspective on the Economy

Chapter 2
Spirituality and Economics

This chapter discusses the relationship between spirituality and economics in a broad context. It shows that mainstream economics is a materialist and reductionist science. It criticizes the core assumptions of mainstream economics—namely, the existence of *Homo Economicus* and the goals of profit maximization, economic efficiency, and economic growth; and shows that these goals lead to an economy that is not only unhealthy for people but is making the planet unsustainable. The chapter makes a case for the development of a spiritually-informed economics. It concludes that by helping to create ecological and human economic practices and policies, spiritually-informed economics can support the flourishing of life on Earth (both human and non-human, present and future).

2.1 Introduction

Mainstream economics is the body of knowledge, including theories and models of economics, which is generally taught by universities worldwide and accepted by a majority of economists as a basis for discussion. It is also referred to as "neoclassical economic orthodoxy," in which markets are moved by an invisible hand, and all actors are rational (Snower, 2020). Like most branches of modern science (Galileo Commission, 2019), mainstream economics is a materialist and reductionist enterprise. It employs a materialist and reductionist conception of

This chapter is a modified version of the author's previously published paper: Zsolnai, L. (2022). Spirituality and Economics. *Journal for the Study of Spirituality, 12*(2), 131–145. https://doi.org/10.1080/20440243.2022.2126136. Copyright © 2022 International Network for the Study of Spirituality and Taylor & Francis, reprinted by permission of Informa UK Limited, trading as Taylor & Francis Ltd, https://www.tandfonline.com on behalf of International Network for the Study of Spirituality and Taylor & Francis.

© The Author(s), under exclusive license to Springer Nature Switzerland AG 2026

L. Zsolnai, *Planet Positive Economy*, Springer Studies in Alternative Economics,
https://doi.org/10.1007/978-3-032-21131-6_2

humanity, presupposing that people have only material needs and desires, and can only be motivated by extrinsic, material incentives, like money.

Materialism is a belief system which claims that "reality" consists of matter and energy, and all phenomena, including mental states and consciousness, are results of material processes. This materialist worldview comes with a value orientation that gives priority to values such as money, possessions, social image, and status. *Reductionism* is a philosophical position claiming that phenomena can be described in terms of other simpler, or more fundamental, phenomena. In this view, a system is nothing more than the sum of its parts.

Materialism and reductionism are meta-economic assumptions on which today's economic discipline is based. The "hard core" of mainstream economics includes the Homo Economicus model, the profit maximization principle, economic efficiency as the main evaluation criterion of economic actions, and economic growth as the principal goal of economic policy. Mainstream economics promotes a strong materialist value orientation and fosters self-interest, greed, competition, and the like. The materialism and reductionism of mainstream economics are not innocent intellectual features of the discipline. The widespread application of materialist and reductionist economic models is producing serious problems in our era, including climate change, biodiversity loss, ecosystem collapse, welfare malaise, and inequalities at national and global levels.

A "spiritually-informed economics" which integrates both the material and the nonmaterial aspects of human existence, assumes that economic actors have a variety of motives and goals, including ethical and spiritual ones. It suggests that the work of a number of economists who are often regarded as marginal to mainstream economics already points to a spiritually-informed view, and that conceptions of economics already embedded in many of the world's religious traditions support such a view.

To understand the concept of "spiritually-informed economics," it is important to note the difference between religion and spirituality. *Religion* is an institutionalized approach to relate humanity to the supernatural or transcendental to find fulfillment, while *spirituality* involves the "multiform search of people for meaning that interconnects them with all living beings and to God or Ultimate Reality" (European SPES Institute, 2021) outside of, or in addition to, a search within traditional institutions. The shared subset of religiousness and spirituality refers to people who are both religious and spiritual. The two disjunct subsets refer to people who are religious but not spiritual, and who are spiritual but not religious (Fig. 2.1).

The main point of this chapter is to provide spiritual foundations to economic thinking. The chapter offers an overview of starting points for debate and is not intended as a single position on what a spiritually-informed economics might look like. It starts from the premise that spirituality in the context of economics means that economic analysis should also consider the nonmaterial aspects of human beings and how they function, including having a sense of transcendence and interconnectedness. It should promote a spiritual value orientation that gives priority to nonmaterialist values (such as community, compassion, friendship, and love) over materialist values (such as money, possessions, social image, and status).

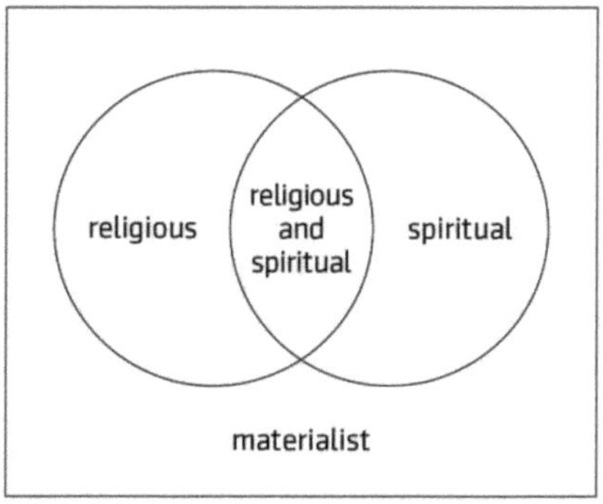

Fig. 2.1 Religiousness versus spirituality. *Source* Author's own creation

2.2 Mainstream Economics as a Materialist and Reductionist Science

Based on its materialist and reductionist assumptions, mainstream economics fails to address current economic, social, and environmental complexities of the Anthropocene era.

Homo Economicus

Mainstream economics uses the concept of Homo Economicus, which assumes that economic agents are rational, self-interest-maximizing beings who only care about their own material benefit. This reductionist approach can be criticized on empirical as well as normative grounds.

Experimental research shows that people do consider the interests of others and care about their self-conception (Sunstein, 2000). Also, in real life, people display what is called "bounded rationality" because their cognitive capacity is poor, and they have only limited information in most situations (Simon, 1982). People also have bounded willpower and sometimes make choices that are not in their own interest (Thaler, 2015). They often make myopic and deficient choices because they lack the ability to predict their future tastes, have fallible memories, and incorrectly evaluate past experiences (Kahneman, 2011). Sen (1977) concludes that if real people behaved in the way that the rational choice model specifies, they would act like "rational fools".

Feminist economists also criticize the Homo Economicus model for presupposing an androcentric, male-biased conception of the human person, the so-called "separative self" (Ferber & Nelson, 1993; Nelson, 2006).

There is a high price of materialism exemplified by the Homo Economicus way of behavior. Extensive psychological studies document that the more people prioritize materialist goals, the lower their personal well-being, and the more likely they are to engage in manipulative, competitive, and ecologically degrading behaviors (Kasser, 2003, 2011).

Profit Maximization

Mainstream economics propagates the claim that profit maximization is the main, and sometimes the only, principle behind economic activity. There are two problems with this. One is related to the nature of profit as the motivation for economic action, while the other is related to profit as the measure of success of economic action (Zsolnai, 2011).

Pure profit-seeking is dangerous when it is the sole motivation for economic activity. It decreases the intrinsic motivation of economic actors, which may lead to a decrease in the quality of the output. Also, it cultivates a strong materialist value orientation, which results in socially insensitive and ethically irresponsible behavior.

The "crowding-out" theory of human motivation shows why profit as the sole motivation is problematic. A monetary reward offered or expected tends to "crowd out" a person's willingness to undertake a task for its own sake if the person's sense of recognition, fairness, or self-determination is negatively affected (Frey, 1997).

Profit is inadequate as the sole measure of the success of economic activities. It does not represent a complete and unbiased evaluation of the result of actions. It reflects the values of the most powerful stakeholders, favors preferences in the "here and now," and presupposes the reducibility of all kinds of values to monetary ones. In addition, it ignores the impact of economic activities on the surrounding community or the environment.

Profit can be used as an indicator of the financial viability of economic activity, but not as an overall criterion of the success of economic actions (Sandel, 2012). To judge the overall value of economic activities, we should use a number of nonfinancial value criteria in addition to financial ones.

Economic Efficiency

Economic efficiency is the central dogma of mainstream economics. It involves the belief that free, competitive markets produce the optimal allocation of resources in society and provide people with maximal aggregate welfare. It is one of the greatest sources of legitimacy for business and economic actions in today's world. The focus on efficiency allows economics to neatly sidestep moral questions concerning what goals and whose interests efficiency serves. However, North (1990) has demonstrated that there is no absolute definition of "efficiency" because the initial distribution of rights and obligations determines what is efficient in a given situation. If that distribution changes, then a different efficient solution emerges.

Economic Growth

Mainstream economics suggests that the ultimate goal of the economic system is growth measured in terms of gross domestic product (GDP), and the main function of national economic policy is to foster this economic growth. Gross domestic product is a monetary measure of the market value of all the final goods and services produced in a specific time period by a national economy. However, there are many problems with using GDP as an indicator. For example, Clair Brown argues that:

> because GDP uses only income to measure economic growth, income has become a country's primary focus. This encourages individuals to focus on what they buy and the country to pay little attention to inequality and sustainability (Brown, 2017: 107).

Other problems with the focus on GDP include the fact that it does not take into account any harm caused to the natural environment. Also, GDP does not capture the state of human health and the level of education in a society. Similarly, GDP does not include the value of household and other unpaid work. Finally, GDP "focuses on flows, not stocks. As a result, an economy can run down its assets yet, at the same time, record high levels of GDP growth" (Natural Capital Committee, 2012).

New Economic Thinking

Realizing the problematic nature of the hard core of mainstream economics, a new kind of economic thinking is emerging, which attempts to free economics from the "iron cage" of utility and profit maximization, market equilibrium, and the standard economic policy toolbox which relies on monetary incentives. New economic thinking includes economics of complex, adaptive systems (Snower, 2020); no-growth economics (Jackson, 2009); doughnut economics for respecting social and planetary boundaries (Raworth, 2017); public value economics (Mazzucato, 2013), and well-being economics (Constanza, 2018).

These are promising directions, but in many cases, they remain imprisoned by the old meta-economic assumptions of materialism and reductionism. New economic thinking currently seems to lack the capacity to make an intellectually credible case for spiritual foundations, perhaps because new economics thinkers lack the courage, awareness, or commitment to engage in discussions about spirituality more directly, and this imposes serious limitations on their endeavor.

2.3 Economic Conceptions of World Religions

Economic conceptions embedded in various world religions challenge the materialist and reductionist worldview of mainstream economics and provide meaningful alternatives to it. They can also give inspiration for the development of a spiritually-informed economics. The following summary of economic conceptions contained in a sample of world religions is provided for illustrative purposes only, since it cannot represent the complexity and richness of these traditions.

Judaism

Judaism considers the role of the entrepreneur to be legitimate and desirable. Entrepreneurs are entitled to a profit in return for fulfilling their function in society. It is an axiom of Judaism that every member of the community has a duty to help the poor and disadvantaged members of the community. Jewish entrepreneurs should give 10%–20% of their profit to charity (Tamari, 1987). The central point of Jewish economic ethics is that one should not cause damage—directly, indirectly, or even accidentally. As a rabbinic principle says: "One has a benefit, and another does not suffer a loss." (For further detail on the economic conception of Judaism, see Epstein, 2000 and Pava, 2011.)

Christianity

According to Christian teaching, a human being is the clearest reflection of God on Earth; thus, human dignity is unconditional. Accordingly, economic decisions and institutions must protect the dignity of all human beings.

Love is at the heart of Christian morality: "Love thy neighbor as thyself." This means that economic actors should give the same weight to the benefits and losses of others as they assign to their own. Justice has three meanings in Catholic Social Teaching. Commutative justice calls for fairness in all agreements and exchanges between individuals and social groups. Distributive justice requires the allocation of income, wealth, and power to aid persons whose basic needs are unmet. Finally, social justice implies the participation of all persons in economic and social life (Mele, 2011).

According to Catholicism, the freedom of business is protected, but the accountability of business for the common good and justice must be assured. The government has an essential moral function: protecting human rights and securing justice for all members of society (U.S. Bishops, 1986). (For further detail on the Catholic conception of economics, see Pope Benedict XVI, 2009; Pope Francis, 2015; Pope Francis, 2020; and Economy of Francesco, 2022. For details on the Protestant conception of economics, see Johnston, 2019).

Islam

Islam requires total submission to the Will of *Allah* from its believers, and that they should follow the laws of *Sharia'h* (Khan, 2011). Islamic economics has three basic tenets: (1) the prohibition of *riba* (i.e., interest or usury) in all financial transactions; (2) wealth redistribution through the levy of *zakat* (a religious alms tax) on all movable wealth; and (3) adherence to Islamic economic norms that include forswearing products and activities deemed *haram* (forbidden) for Muslims, such as drinking alcohol, eating pork, gambling, and using pornography (Khan, 2011: 141).

The most developed part of Islamic economics is Islamic banking and finance, where the financier takes a direct equity stake in a venture rather than offering a fully collateralized, interest-based loan (Khan, 2011). (For more on Islamic economics, see Kuran, 2004).

Hinduism

Hindu economic thought is based on the ancient Indian philosophical tradition characterized by *advaita* (nonduality) consciousness. It absorbs all dualities in the grand continuum of cosmic experience across space and time. Polarities or opposites exist in this scheme not as disparate fragments of reality; rather, they are deeply interconnected in time, space, and essence against that backdrop. Hindu spirituality requires that actors engage in Higher Wisdom and provide disinterested service to all beings (Mukherjee, 2011).

The Indian leader, Mahatma Gandhi, followed the philosophy of advaita, which states that the world is one, there is no division between subject and object, and that there is unity between humanity and nature. He recognized the basic right of all to live and blossom. Greed can never be satisfied, but nature produces enough for everyone if we take only what is enough for us. All living beings have an equal right to exist on this planet. The ultimate goal of human life is the attainment of *moksha*, i.e., liberation from all ills and from rebirth (Kumaria, 2003).

Gandhi insisted on limiting wants so that the impact of human life on nature is minimized. He emphasized the importance of living close to the land. His aim was not only political freedom for India but also freedom from poverty, inequality, the caste system, and fear (Kumaria, 2003). (For more on Hindu economic views, see Mukherjee, 2022, and Mukherjee & Zsolnai, 2022.)

Buddhism

Buddhist economics is based on the Buddhist way of life, the main goal of which is liberation from all suffering. *Nirvana* is the final state, which can be approached by want negation and purification of the human character (Schumacher, 1973). The central values of Buddhist economics are simplicity, nonviolence, interdependence, and "no-self" (*anatta*).

For Buddhists, the optimal pattern of consumption involves achieving human satisfaction with the least material consumption. The most rational way of organizing economic life is by producing local resources to meet local needs. Dependence on imports from afar and the consequent need for exporting is uneconomic, and justifiable only in exceptional cases. Buddhist economics represents a "Middle Way" between the modern growth economy and traditional nongrowth economy (Schumacher, 1973). It seeks the most appropriate path of development that includes all aspects of human and ecological well-being, treating all people the same, and caring for all beings (Brown, 2017). (For more on Buddhist economics, see Payutto, 1992, and Zsolnai & Ims, 2006.)

Confucianism

Tao is a Chinese concept that represents the way of equilibrium and harmony among the myriad things of the universe. It is based on the belief that two basic forces exist in the universe: yin and yang. *Yin* is the yielding, cooperative force. *Yang* is the active, competitive force.

In the Confucian economy, two basic values play decisive roles, the inner equilibrium of individuals and social harmony. At the microeconomic level, the following yin and yang pairs are balanced: (1) public interest *versus* self-interest; (2) morality *versus* profit; (3) want negation *versus* want satisfaction; (4) cooperation *versus* competition; and (5) leisure *versus* work (Sun, 1986). At the macroeconomic level, the following yin and yang pairs are balanced: (1) the poor *versus* the

Table 2.1 Economic conceptions of various world religions

	Basic values	Economic means
Judaism	Cause no harm, solidarity	Constraints on profit-making, charity
Christianity	Love, justice	Responsible enterprises, duties of the government
Islam	Total submission to the Will of *Allah*, following the laws of *Sharia'h*	Prohibition of interest; wealth redistribution through religious alms tax; forswearing forbidden products and activities
Hinduism	Nonduality consciousness, selfless service to all	Work and decent livelihood for everybody, community-based enterprises
Buddhism	Simplicity, nonviolence, interdependence, no-self	Reduced consumption, using local resources, and ecological conservation
Confucianism	Inner equilibrium of the individual, social harmony	Balancing the yin and yang forces at the micro and macro levels

Source Author's own creation

rich; (2) labor *versus* capital; (3) the public sector *versus* the private sector; (4) the planning system *versus* the market system; (5) stagnation *versus* growth; and (6) full employment *versus* price stability (Sun, 1986). (For more on the economic conception of Confucianism, see Allinson, 2011, and Rothlin, 2016.)

The main characteristics of the economic conceptions of the world religions noted above are summarized in Table 2.1.

2.4 Toward a Spiritually-Informed Economics

To be relevant and useful in today's world, mainstream economics needs to be expanded and redirected. It needs to go beyond its materialist and reductionist meta-economic assumptions and move from a strict materialistic value orientation to a more holistic, spiritual value orientation. Freeing mainstream economics from materialism and reductionism and moving towards a spiritually-informed economics needs to include the following main developments.

Capturing the Whole Spectrum of Human Existence

Humanity's outdated, purely materialistic conception of mainstream economics—the model of Homo Economicus—should be replaced by a more complex model that captures the nonmaterial aspects as well as the material aspects of human existence. The emerging *Homo Spiritualis* model accepts the importance of people's material needs and desires, but also acknowledges nonmaterial needs and desires, such as for love, friendship, care, connectedness, the search for meaning, and self-actualization (Kaufman, 2020).

Bouckaert (2011) writes that according to the *Homo Spiritualis* model, people are not striving for preference satisfaction and utility maximization but are aware of being related to others. This interexistence is irreducible and prior to group interest or collective welfare. The spirit in human beings is an awareness where they feel themselves related to all other beings and to Being itself. It transforms the materialistic body-mind ego into a compassionate and responsible spiritual self. This conception has some resonance with the ideas of Rabindranath Tagore and Swami Vivekananda, who were grounded in the Vedanta philosophy that upholds a spiritual model of humanity, the so-called "Amritasya Putrah" (Children of Immortality).

Mainstream economics employs a simplified picture of the economy. The economy consists of individuals/households, firms, and the state, and only monetized transactions are considered among them. However, in reality, the economic system is far more complex. Kornai (1990) identified four basic coordination mechanisms that play a decisive role in the working of economic systems. These mechanisms are market coordination, bureaucratic coordination, ethical coordination, and aggressive coordination. Combinations of these coordination mechanisms occur. But the combinations of different coordination mechanisms are not always stable. Market coordination may "crowd-out" ethical coordination. However, it is possible to develop institutional arrangements that ensure ethical coordination "crowds-in" market coordination (Bowles, 2016). In this way, the positive effects of ethics and the market can be combined.

Mainstream economics suggests using extrinsic motivation (monetary incentives) in economic action. This creates numerous malfunctions of the system, including declines in productivity and quality of work, loss of team spirit, and increasing stress and ill-being at the workplace (Frey, 1997). However, self-determination theory (Ryan & Deci, 2017) claims that the motivation for people's choices in the absence of external influences and distractions can lead to exceptionally good results. This theory promotes self-motivated and self-determined human behavior and demonstrates the salutary effects of human autonomy, including a prosocial orientation and psychological health, in the workplace and beyond. If economic arrangements give freedom and autonomy to people and help to activate their intrinsic motivation, then value creation processes can be boosted both in material and nonmaterial terms.

Redefining Economics as a Science of the Livelihood of People

The subject matter of mainstream economics is defined as the production, distribution, and consumption of goods and services. In contrast, Polanyi (1977) suggested that the central task of economics should be studying the livelihood arrangements that make it possible for people to survive in interaction with the natural environment and their social communities. This broader, substantive view (which goes back to Aristotle's original notion of *oikonomia*), allows economists to study both market and non-market systems and to move beyond the formal, materialist conception of economizing.

Spiritually-informed economics focuses on the livelihood of people instead of profit-making. This implies that the performance of the economic system should be

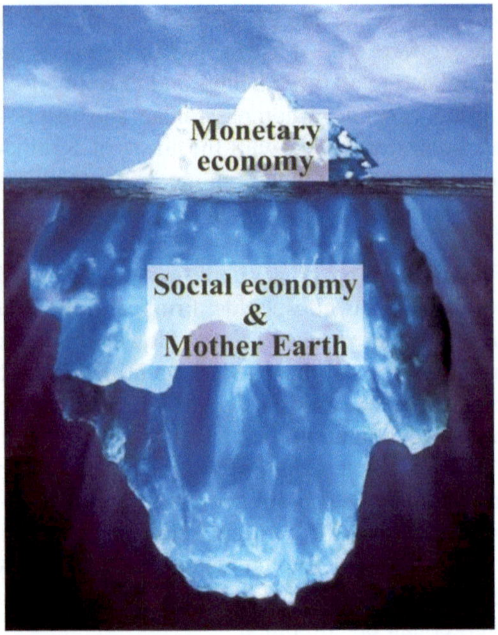

Fig. 2.2 The whole economic Iceberg. *Source* Author's own creation

measured by metrics other than GDP. These new metrics should reflect the state of the environment, the distribution of resources among people, and the physical, mental, and spiritual health of people.

Mainstream economics addresses only the monetized activities of society. However, an economic system is much larger than the monetized sphere of society. It contains the nonmonetized, unpaid work of society members and the life-supporting functions of nature (Zsolnai, 2013). The whole "economic iceberg" should be considered when studying the value creation processes of the economy (Fig. 2.2).

The submerged part of the economic iceberg is much bigger than the monetary tip, as the social economy and the myriad life-supporting functions of natural ecosystems constitute a considerable part of the total economic system (Constanza, 1997).

Mainstream economics commits the error of "pars pro toto." This means that instead of considering the whole, it is focused on only a small part of the total economic functioning. In this way, the theories and recommendations of mainstream economics are partial and can be misleading in many cases.

Promoting Frugal Production and Consumption

Today, the most advanced economies are functioning in huge ecological overshoot and use far more environmental resources and space than their fair "earth share" (Global Footprint Network, 2022). This implies that production and consumption of materials and energy in such advanced economies should be radically reduced.

Daly (2008) argues that frugality should precede efficiency if we are to achieve a state of sustainability, because efficiency alone is not an adequate solution for downsizing the material part of our overgrown economies. He notes:

> An improvement in efficiency by itself is equivalent to having a larger supply of the factor whose efficiency increased. More uses of the cheaper factor will be found. We will end up consuming more of the resource than before, albeit more efficiently. Scale continues to grow (Daly, 2008: 222).

Frugality leads to the revival of the corresponding logic of sufficiency (Princen, 2005). Frugality and sufficiency require:

> more substantive organizational forms that radically alter the underlying structure of currently dominating configurations of formal economizing. This means (. . .) introducing smaller scale, locally adaptable, culturally diverse modes of substantive economic activities (Zsolnai, 2002: 661).

Developing Holistic Measures of Value and Well-Being

Mainstream economics tends to reduce every kind of value to a one-dimensional measure—namely, market price. This leads to difficulties and problems because nonmonetary values like ecological, aesthetic, ethical, and spiritual values cannot be translated into market prices. In real-life situations, the application of the one-dimensional value calculations of mainstream economics often result in the neglect of vitally important values.

A spiritually-informed economics needs to develop holistic measures that reflect the multidimensional nature of value. The total value of an object or process can be better captured in terms of a variety of factors that include financial, social, and ecological values. These values cannot be aggregated but form a multicomponent vector. If x is an object or process, then the value of x can be schematically expressed as follows: $V(x) = [F(x), S(x), E(x)]$ where F(), S(), and E() are financial, social, and ecological value functions, respectively. To compare value vectors of this kind is not easy, but some heuristic rules can be developed for making reasonable economic choices between them (Bogetoft & Pruzan, 1991).

Well-being is also a multidimensional phenomenon. It is related to Aristotle's conception of *eudaimonia*, which is usually translated as "flourishing." It involves the fulfillment of one's human capacities (Haybron, 2020). Well-being reflects a convergence of good human life (physical, mental, and spiritual), equity and fairness, a peaceful community, and supportive social relationships within a flourishing natural environment (Shrivastava & Zsolnai, 2022).

From a spiritual perspective, the main goal of economic policy is to provide conditions for the flourishing of human and nonhuman life. This policy goal involves acknowledging the intrinsic value of nature and focusing on human capabilities. However, mainstream economics does not accept the intrinsic value of nature. It suggests valuing environmental goods and services on the basis of market value determined by competing economic actors. The value of nature is often calculated by using the "willingness to pay" principle or shadow price techniques. But the value of natural entities cannot be calculated merely based on their utility to humans. Price is a poor means of assessing the true value of natural entities and often leads to misguided decisions (McDaniel & Gowdy, 2000).

In his encyclical letter *Laudato si'*, Pope Francis urges acceptance of the intrinsic value of nature and the expression of appreciation for it because natural creatures and ecosystems

> have an intrinsic value independent of their usefulness. Each organism, as a creature of God, is good and admirable in itself; the same is true of the harmonious ensemble of organisms existing in a defined space and functioning as a system (Pope Francis, 2015: §140).

Accepting the intrinsic value of nature implies recognizing that there is no algorithmic solution to the allocation problems of natural resources. Ecological, social, and economic values are incommensurable (Martinez-Allier et al., 1998), so decisions and policies require qualitative and multiperspective considerations.

While mainstream economics accepts formal rights and negative freedoms, the capability approach championed by Sen (1999) and Nussbaum (2000) asserts that the freedom of humans to achieve well-being is of primary importance, and human well-being can be understood in terms of people's capabilities and functioning. In this view, economic development can be understood as the expansion of real or substantive freedoms that people enjoy (Robeyns & Byskov, 2021).

2.5 Conclusion

The list above of possible directions toward a spiritually-informed economics is far from complete. In addition to capturing the full spectrum of human existence, redefining economics as a science of the livelihood of people, promoting frugal production and consumption, and developing holistic measures of value and well-being, further directions can be added to the agenda for the development of a spiritually-informed economics.

The civil economy tradition, which focuses on relationality and reciprocity among economic actors and emphasizes the importance of gratuity and a common good orientation, is an important direction (Bruni & Zamagni, 2017). Another is the consideration of ecological footprinting and rightsizing of economic activities to respect the global biophysical boundaries of human functioning (Brown & Timmerman, 2015). Finally, it is very promising for a spiritually-informed economics that feminist economists emphasize the importance of mothering, care, and relatedness in economic settings. Mansbridge (1990) favors the coincidence of duty and love with self-interest. She argues that both empathic feelings and moral commitments are embedded in a social context. Arrangements are required that generate some return for nonself-interested behavior to create an "ecological niche" for sustaining such behavior (Mansbridge, 1990: 134).

Mainstream economics as a profession suffers from serious problems (DeMartino & McCloskey, 2016; Rona & Zsolnai, 2017). By engaging with spirituality and including the non-material aspects of human existence, economic thinking can expand its scope and reorient its value direction to become more realistic and effective in today's world. In helping to create ecological and human economic practices and policies, spiritually-informed economics may become a force for good by supporting the flourishing of life on Earth—both human and nonhuman, present and future.

References

Allinson, R. (2011). Taoism and Confucianism. In L. Bouckaert & L. Zsolnai (Eds.), *The Palgrave handbook of spirituality and business* (pp. 95–102). Palgrave-Macmillan.

Bogetoft, P. & Pruzan, P. (1991). *Planning with multiple criteria: Investigation, communication, choice*. Elsevier.

Bouckaert, L. (2011). Personalism. In L. Bouckaert & L. Zsolnai (Eds.), *The Palgrave handbook of spirituality and business* (pp. 155–162). Palgrave-Macmillan.

Bowles, S. (2016). *The moral economy: Why good incentives are no substitute for good citizens*. Yale University Press.

Brown, C. (2017). *Buddhist economics—An enlightened approach to the dismal science*. Bloomsbury Press.

Brown, P. G. & Timmerman, P. (Eds.) (2015). *Ecological economics for the athropocene*. Columbia University Press.

Bruni, L. & Zamagni, S. (2017). *Civil economy. Another idea of the market*. Columbia University Press.

Constanza, R. (1997). The value of the world's ecosystem services and natural capital. *Nature*, *387*(6630), 253–260.

Constanza, R. (2018). Toward a sustainable wellbeing economy. *Solutions*, *9*(2). https://thesolutionsjournal.com/toward-sustainable-wellbeing-economy/. Accessed December 9, 2025.

Daly, H. (2008). Frugality first. In L. Bouckaert, H. Opdebeeck, & L. Zsolnai (Eds.), *Frugality: Rebalancing material and spiritual values in economic life* (pp. 207–226). Peter Lang Publishing.

DeMartino, G. F. II. & McCloskey, D. N. (Eds.) (2016). *The Oxford handbook of professional economic ethics*. Oxford University Press.

Economy of Francesco (2022). https://francescoeconomy.org/. Accessed March 20, 2025.

Epstein, E. M. (2000). Contemporary Jewish perspectives on business ethics: The contributions of Meir Tamari and Moses L Pava—A review essay. *Business Ethics Quarterly*, *10*(2), 523–542.

European SPES Institute 2021. http://eurospes.org/. Accessed December 7, 2024.

Ferber, M. A. & Nelson, J. A. (Eds.) (1993). *Beyond economic man*. The University of Chicago Press.

Frey, B. (1997). *Not just for the money*. Edward Elgar.

Galileo Commission (2019). *Beyond a materialist worldview. Towards an expanded science*. https://galileocommission.org/report/. Accessed March 17, 2025.

Global Footprint Network (2022). https://www.footprintnetwork.org/. Accessed August 18, 2025.

Haybron, D. (2020). Happiness. *The Stanford Encyclopedia of Philosophy*. https://plato.stanford.edu/archives/sum2020/entries/happiness. Accessed March 17, 2025.

Jackson, T. (2009). *Prosperity without growth? The transition to a sustainable economy*. Routledge.

Johnston, C. F. (2019). A protestant rethinking of economics for a healthier world. *American Journal of Economics and Sociology*, *78*(2), 363–408.

Kahneman, D. (2011). *Thinking, fast and slow*. Farrar, Straus and Giroux.

Kasser, T. (2003). *The high price of materialism*. MIT Press.

Kasser, T. (2011). Materialistic value-orientation. In L. Bouckaert & L. Zsolnai (Eds.), *The Palgrave handbook of spirituality and business* (pp. 204–211). Palgrave-Macmillan.
Kaufman, S. B. (2020). *Transcend. The new science of self-actualization*. Penguin, Random House.
Khan, F. (2011). Islamic economics. In L. Bouckaert & L. Zsolnai (Eds.), *The Palgrave handbook of spirituality and business* (pp. 138–146). Palgrave-Macmillan.
Kornai, J. (1990). The affinity between ownership forms and coordination mechanisms. The common experience of reform in socialist countries. *Journal of Economic Perspectives, 4*(3), 131–147.
Kumaria, P. (2003). Nature and man: Gandhian concept of deep ecology. *Anasakti, 2*.
Kuran, T. (2004). *Islam and Mammon: The economic predicaments of Islamism*. Princeton University Press.
Mansbridge, J. J. (1990). On the relation of altruism and self-interest. In J. J. Mansbridge (Ed.), *Beyond self-interest* (pp. 133–143). The University of Chicago Press.
Martinez-Allier, J., Munda, G., & O'Neill, J. (1998). Weak comparability of values as a foundation for ecological economics. *Ecological Economics, 26*(3), 277–286.
Mazzucato, M. (2013). *The entrepreneurial state: Debunking public vs. private myths in risk and innovation*. Anthem Press.
McDaniel, C. & Gowdy, J. (2000). *Paradise for sale: Regaining sustainability—A parable of nature*. University of California Press.
Mele, D. (2011). Catholic social teaching. In L. Bouckaert & L. Zsolnai (Eds.), *The Palgrave handbook of spirituality and business* (pp. 118–128). Palgrave-Macmillan.
Mukherjee, S. (2011). Indian management philosophy. In L. Bouckaert & L. Zsolnai (Eds.), *The Palgrave handbook of spirituality and business* (pp. 80–87). Palgrave-Macmillan.
Mukherjee, S. (2022). Looking east. In *Indian wisdom for modern management*. Peter Lang Academic Publishers.
Mukherjee, S. & Zsolnai, L. (Eds.) (2022). *Global perspectives on Indian spirituality and management. The legacy of S.K. Chakraborty*. Springer.
Natural Capital Committee (2012). https://www.gov.uk
Nelson, J. A. (2006). *Economics for humans*. The University of Chicago Press.
North, D. (1990). *Institutions, institutional change and economic performance*. Cambridge University Press.
Nussbaum, M. (2000). *Women and human development: The capabilities approach*. Cambridge University Press.
Pava, M. (2011). *Jewish ethics in a post-madoff world: A case for optimism*. Palgrave.
Payutto, P.A. (1992). *Buddhist economics: A middle way for the market place*. http://pioneer.netserv.chula.ac.th/~sprapant/Buddhism/buddhist_econ.html. Accessed March 20, 2022.
Polanyi, K. (1977). *The livelihood of man*. Academic Press.
Pope Benedict, XVI. (2009). https://www.vatican.va/content/benedict-xvi/en/encyclicals/documents/hf_ben-xvi_enc_20090629_caritas-in-veritate.html. Accessed March 20, 2022.
Pope Francis. (2015). Laudato si'. https://www.vatican.va/content/francesco/en/encyclicals/documents/papa-francesco_20150524_enciclica-laudato-si.html. Accessed March 17, 2025.
Pope Francis. (2020). https://www.vatican.va/content/francesco/en/encyclicals/documents/papa-francesco_20201003_enciclica-fratelli-tutti.html. Accessed March 27, 2025.
Princen, T. (2005). *The logic of sufficiency*. MIT Press.
Raworth, K. (2017). *Doughnut economics: Seven ways to think like a 21st-century economist*. Chelsea Green Publishing.
Robeyns, I. & Byskov, M. F. (2021). The capability approach. *The Stanford Encyclopedia of Philosophy*. https://plato.stanford.edu/archives/win2021/entries/capability-approach/. Accessed September 3, 2021.
Rona, P. & Zsolnai, L. (Eds.) (2017). *Economics as a moral science*. Springer.
Rothlin, S. (2016). *International business ethics. Focus on China*. Springer.

Ryan, R. M. & Deci, E. L. (2017). *Self-determination theory: Basic psychological needs in motivation, development, and wellness*. The Guilford Press.
Sandel, M. (2012). *What money can't buy: The moral limits of markets*. Farrar, Straus and Giroux.
Schumacher, E. F. (1973). *Small is beautiful*. Abacus.
Sen, A. (1977). Rational fools: A critique of the behavioral foundations of economic theory. *Philosophy & Public Affairs*, *6*(4), 317–344.
Sen, A. (1999). *Development as freedom*. Knopf.
Simon, H. A. (1982). *Models of bounded rationality*. The MIT Press.
Shrivastava, P. & Zsolnai, L. (2022). Wellbeing-oriented organizations: Connecting human flourishing with ecological regeneration. *Business Ethics, the Environment, and Responsibility 31*(2), 386–397.
Snower, D. (2020, December 28). Economics nears a new paradigm. *Evonomics*. https://evonomics.com/why-behavioral-economics-cant-fix-a-broken-discipline/. Accessed May 24, 2022.
Sun, L.-T. (1986). Confucianism and the economic order of Taiwan. *International Journal of Social Economics*, *13*(6), 3–53.
Sunstein, C. R. (Ed.) (2000). *Behavioral law and economics*. Cambridge University Press.
Tamari, M. (1987). *With all your possessions: Jewish ethics and economic life*. The Free Press.
Thaler, R. (2015). *Misbehaving. The making of behavioral economics*. W. W. Norton & Company.
U.S. Bishops (1986). Economic Justice for All. *Origins*, *24*, 1986.
Zsolnai, L. (2002). Green business or community economy? *International Journal of Social Economics*, *29*(8), 652–662.
Zsolnai, L. (2011). Redefining economic reason. In H. Opdebeeck & L. Zsolnai (Eds.), *Spiritual humanism and economic wisdom, Antwerp/Apeldoom* (pp. 187–200). Garant.
Zsolnai, L. (2013). The importance of meta-economics. In H. Opdebeeck (Ed.), *Responsible economics. E. F. Schumacher and his legacy for the 21st century* (pp. 23–32). Peter Lang Academic Publishers.
Zsolnai, L. & Ims, K. (Eds.). (2006). *Business within limits: Deep ecology and Buddhist economics*. Peter Lang Publishers.

Chapter 3
The Economics of Pope Francis

This chapter analyses the development of Pope Francis' economic views. First, it briefly shows the relationship of St. Francis of Assisi, who inspired Pope Francis, to the economy and then explores—among other documents—the main economic messages of the papal encyclical Laudato si'. Finally, it presents Pope Francis' "The Economy of Francesco" initiative and discusses further opportunities for development.

3.1 St. Francis of Assisi's Views on the Economy

Pope Francis chose St. Francis of Assisi as his role model for his papacy. It is worth studying the relationship of St. Francis to the economy because his views are echoed in the economic conceptions of Pope Francis.

It is well known that St. Francis of Assisi had a hostile attitude toward money, material possessions, and the market. His ideal was a simple, property-free, peaceful community life without market activities (Zsolnai, 2018). Today, this attitude may seem like a kind of antieconomics, but it is worth knowing that for most of human history, economic activities were organized without the operation of the market (Gowdy, 1997).

The views of St. Francis of Assisi are in line with a substantive understanding of the economy, where economic activities are ordered to satisfy the material needs of human communities in harmony with nature.

St. Francis of Assisi represented and promoted material poverty. He did this so that people could live a God-centered life that created an opportunity for spiritual

---

This chapter is a modified version of the author's previously published paper: Zsolnai, L. (2025). The Economics of Pope Francis, The Way, 64(2) 23–34. (https://www.theway.org.uk). Used with the permission of the copyright owner.

© The Author(s), under exclusive license to Springer Nature Switzerland AG 2026

L. Zsolnai, *Planet Positive Economy*, Springer Studies in Alternative Economics,
https://doi.org/10.1007/978-3-032-21131-6_3

growth and development. The extent of his asceticism can be criticized, but in any case, a simple lifestyle is a prerequisite for human happiness and well-being.

St. Francis of Assisi advocated reducing material desires to the minimum possible. Minimizing material consumption is associated with many advantages for the individual, the community, and nature (Zsolnai, 2017).

St. Francis of Assisi supported the idea of self-sufficient communities. A community economy is an organization that engages in substantive, nonmonetary activities, the main goal of which is to ensure sufficient material sustenance for community members. Community economies primarily use local resources and strive for self-sufficiency—especially in the areas of energy production and food supply. They practice ecological sustainability by respecting the carrying capacity of the natural environment (Douthwaite, 1996; Veress, 2023).

St. Francis of Assisi's vision was a *universal brotherhood* of humans and nonhuman beings based on God's infinite love for all the creatures. This ideal appears in today's economic and ethics discourse as "The Commonwealth of Life" (Brown, 2015).

The human economy is embedded in the ecological systems of nature. According to the ecological ethics of St. Francis of Assisi, we should approach natural beings with compassion and love, and our economy should reflect this attitude.

3.2 The Economic Views of Pope Francis

In one of his first apostolic exhortations, *Evangelii Gaudium* (Francis, 2013), Pope Francis sharply criticized the economic practices that deify money and pursue growth. He urged a radical rethinking of capitalism and the modern business enterprise.

In a provocative book entitled *This Economy Kills* (Tornielli & Galeazzi, 2015), Pope Francis expressed his view that the way the economy works today is deeply against life because it pushes millions of people into poverty and destroys nature. In the eyes of many, the words of Pope Francis may seem exaggerated, but calmer, scientific analysis shows that the functioning of our contemporary economy is inherently intertwined with—often merciless—violence against human beings and nature (Zsolnai, 2021).

In his encyclical *Laudato si'* (Francis, 2015), Pope Francis calls on people to undergo an ecological conversion. The encyclical urges all of us to feel personal responsibility for the fate of the Earth, for the well-being of all our fellow human beings, and for the life chances of future generations. The encyclical marks a turning point in Christian thinking about nature and the relationship between the economy and nature.

In the encyclical, Francis (2015) announces new views that have profound implications for economic theory and practice. The key ideas are practicing moderation and recognizing the intrinsic value of nature.

The Importance of Moderation

The encyclical strongly criticizes the dominant "use and throw away" culture of modern societies, which "generates so much waste because of the disordered desire to consume more than what is really necessary" (Francis, 2015: §123). It urges us to strive to "modify [...] consumption, develop [...] an economy of waste disposal and recycling, protect [...] certain species and plan [...] a diversified agriculture and the rotation of crops" (Francis, 2015: §180).

Pope Francis is worried because "we have too many means and only a few insubstantial ends" (Francis, 2015, §203). He encourages us to develop "more sober lifestyles while reducing their energy consumption and improving [...] efficiency." (Francis, 2015: §193). He is convinced that "a decrease in the pace of production and consumption can at times give rise to another form of progress and development" (Francis, 2015: §191).

Pope Francis underlines that Christian spirituality involves "an alternative understanding of the quality of life, and encourages a prophetic and contemplative lifestyle, one capable of deep enjoyment free of the obsession with consumption. [...] We need to take up an ancient lesson found in different religious traditions and also in the Bible. It is the conviction that 'less is more'" (Francis, 2015: §222). We should return to a lifestyle "which allows us to stop and appreciate the small things, to be grateful for the opportunities which life affords us, to be spiritually detached from what we possess, and not to succumb to sadness for what we lack" (Francis, 2015: §222). Happiness requires "knowing how to limit some needs" (Francis, 2015: §223).

Ecological economics has revealed that consumption activities in modern societies have a negative impact on natural ecosystems and reduce the chances of future generations living a decent life (Daly, 1996; Georgescu-Roegen, 1971). Western humanity currently functions in a state of overconsumption, and a significant reduction of the current level of consumption would be needed to return to a sustainable level of functioning.

The ecological footprint data for most developed Western economies show that the latter's use of natural resources exceeds the fair and sustainable share of the earth's ecological goods and services by orders of magnitude—in many cases, by 200%–500% (Global Footprint Network, 2023).

According to Daly (1996), the main task of our time is to achieve ecological moderation—that is, to reduce the scale of the economy relative to ecosystems and to change the present uneconomic growth paradigm, which increases social costs more than benefits and thus makes us poorer, not richer.

Frugality requires reconciling and balancing material and spiritual values in the economy and our personal lives (Bouckaert et al., 2008). This means following the logic of "sufficiency" instead of maximizing production and consumption. The realization of frugality requires smaller-scale, locally adaptive, and culturally diverse forms of economic organization (Zsolnai, 2002).

The Intrinsic Value of Nature

In *Laudato si'*, Pope Francis calls on us to recognize the intrinsic value of nature and to express our love for her. Natural beings and ecosystems "have an intrinsic value independent of their usefulness. Each organism, as a creature of God, is good and admirable in itself; the same is true of the harmonious ensemble of organisms existing in a defined space and functioning as a system" (Francis, 2015: §140).

The encyclical emphasizes that "environmental protection cannot be assured solely on the basis of financial calculations of costs and benefits. The environment is one of those goods that cannot be adequately safeguarded or promoted by market forces" (Francis, 2015: §190).

Contemporary environmental ethics supports Pope Francis' position. The starting principle of environmental ethics is that all living things have intrinsic value, regardless of their usefulness to humans. Living things are valuable in and for themselves and cannot be mere means for the realization of human projects (Fox, 1990; Zsolnai, 2011).

Pope Francis warns that Jesus "invited us to contemplate the lilies of the field and the birds of the air" (Francis, 2015: 226). American ecologist and anthropologist Bateson (1972, 1979) reached a similar conclusion based on modern science.

According to Bateson, we can rebuild love and gratitude for communities of living organisms through close connection with them. Personal and active engagement with the world of nature and art—which goes beyond the rational—can lead to this. Poetry, painting, dance, music, humor, metaphors, religion, and the study of nature provide an opportunity to experience the wisdom that has accumulated over millions of years of evolution (Charlton, 2008).

Fraternity and Social Friendship

In 2020, on the feast of St. Francis of Assisi, Francis (2020) published the encyclical *Fratelli tutti* on fraternity and social friendship, using St. Francis's own words to describe our universal brotherhood and sisterhood. In 2019, the meeting of Pope Francis with Ahmad el-Tayeb, Grand Imam of al-Azhar, in Abu Dhabi served as an inspiration for this encyclical.

The encyclical calls for human fraternity and social solidarity and is a plea to reject wars. It focuses on contemporary social and economic problems and proposes fraternity as a guiding principle for a new world where all countries are part of a larger human family (Francis, 2020).

Pope Francis uses the parable of the Good Samaritan. He says this parable is an "ever new" call from Jesus to "rediscover our vocation as citizens of our respective nations and of the entire world, builders of a new social bond" (Francis, 2020: §66). The parable invites us to introspect our inner struggle between our own security and personal sacrifices required by charity. The parable "speaks to us of an essential and often forgotten aspect of our common humanity: we were created for a fulfilment that can only be found in love" (Francis, 2020: §68). Pope Francis adds: "All of us have a responsibility for the wounded" and "[w]e have the space we need for co-responsibility in creating and putting into place new processes and changes" (Francis, 2020: §77).

In *Fratelli tutti*, Pope Francis states that universal brotherhood is possible, but requires "a decisive commitment to devising effective means to this end" (Francis, 2020: §180). He criticizes isolationism, nationalism, a global economy that promotes individual interests, limitless consumption, wastefulness, the lack of concern for the environment, and a throwaway culture.

In the encyclical, Pope Francis says: "Social friendship and universal fraternity necessarily call for an acknowledgement of the worth of every human person, always and everywhere" (Francis, 2020: §106). He emphasizes that individualism "does not make us more free, more equal, more fraternal" (Francis, 2020: §105) and that what is needed is a "universal love" (Francis, 2020: §106) which promotes the dignity of every human being.

The encyclical warns against selfishness in the economy, and against financial speculation, which "continues to wreak havoc." For Pope Francis, the COVID-19 pandemic has shown that not everything can be resolved by market capitalism and that human dignity must be put back at the centre.

Fratelli tutti accepts the right to property, but states that this right "can only be considered a secondary natural right" (Francis, 2020: §120) when compared to human dignity. Pope Francis attempts to reorient the right to property as a responsibility for the care of the whole planet. This suggests the positive meaning of the right to property. The owners care for and cultivate their property in such a way that it can contribute to the good of all. The encyclical argues that the right to private property should be accompanied by the prior principle of "subordination of all private property to the universal destination of the earth's goods, and thus the right of all to their use" (Francis, 2020: §120).

This vision of the economy aligns with new thinking in business ethics, which promotes working models in which economic value creation is subordinated to enhancing human well-being and planetary sustainability (Shrivastava & Zsolnai, 2022, Zsolnai et al., 2023).

3.3 "The Economy of Francesco" Initiative

One of Pope Francis' last initiatives was the "The Economy of Francesco" project. Inspired by St. Francis of Assisi, the project aims to build a new economy based on friendship with nature and promoting peace. The task is to transform today's violent and destructive economy into one that serves life in every respect (EoF, 2023).

The Economy of Francesco initiative is supported by world-renowned economists, including Stefano Zamagni, professor at the University of Bologna; Luigino Bruni, professor at the LUMSA University in Rome and Sophia University, Helen Alford, dean of the Pontifical University of St. Thomas Aquinas—Angelicum and president of The Pontifical Academy of Social Sciences; Kate Raworth, a researcher at the University of Oxford, and Vandana Shiva, director of the Navdanya Research Foundation for Science, Technology and Ecology in India.

The Economy of Francesco initiative aims to capture the imagination of young generations. It primarily calls for the participation of economists, business entrepreneurs, and social change-makers under the age of 35 in joint thinking and action aimed at building a new economy (EoF, 2023).

The initiative of Pope Francis is connected with the civil economy paradigm, which follows an ancient Italian tradition of seeing the market as a place centered on civil virtues. The ideal of the civil economy integrates three basic principles of social order: the principle of the exchange of equivalents, the principle of redistribution, and the principle of reciprocity. The concerted outcome of these three principles, represented by the market, the state, and civil society, can produce efficiency, equity, and public happiness in a modern society (Bruni & Zamagni, 2008, 2016).

The first world meeting of The Economy of Francesco initiative took place on September 22–24, 2022, in Assisi, with the participation of Pope Francis and the Bishop of Assisi, Domenico Sorrentino. More than 1000 young Christian and non-Christian professionals and social activists from more than 50 countries gathered there. The work was carried out in thematic groups focusing on the key problems with today's economies. The thematic groups were: (1) policies for happiness, (2) energy and poverty, (3) life and lifestyle, (4) business and peace, (5) women and the economy, (6) transformation of business, (7) work and care, (8) CO_2 emissions and inequality, (9) management and giving, (10) mission and profit, (11) agriculture and social justice, and (12) finance and humanity (EoF, 2023).

The Business Ethics Center of the Corvinus University of Budapest organized a workshop at the Assisi meeting entitled "New business models in the service of human fulfillment and ecological regeneration" (BEC, 2023). The workshop discussed the deep existential challenges facing humanity today (climate crisis, the radical decline of biodiversity, collapse of ecosystems, and drastic increase in social inequalities and migration) and presented innovative business and social models that simultaneously support human well-being and ecological regeneration.

The Economy of Francesco initiative continues in many forms worldwide. These projects include the Economy of Francesco Academy, the Economy of Francesco School, the Economy of Francesco Thematic Villages, and the Economy of Francesco Hubs (EoF, 2023).

3.4 Summary and Outlook

It is customary to refer to economics as a "dismal science." But it does not have to be that way. Economics can also be an "angelic science" if it serves the real needs of people and supports the preservation of the created world. This is what Pope Francis calls on us to appreciate.

Sustainable development cannot be reconciled with today's ecologically destructive business practices that escape their own social responsibility. Earth conservation and social progress require the creation of new economic organizations that respect nature, take into account the interests of future generations, and benefit all members of society (Zsolnai et al., 2023).

Social and technological innovation plays a decisive role in the desirable transformation of the economy. Environmentally sensitive and ecologically regenerative business solutions can be developed in close cooperation with local communities and non-governmental organizations, where the main goal is not to obtain the greatest possible profit but to promote socioeconomic wellbeing. Democratic social participation can facilitate the creation of new types of community-oriented economic activity (O'Higgins & Zsolnai, 2017).

We need to develop an ecological awareness that carefully and effectively translates into action the belief that we are all children of God and leads to the sharing of the wealth of the Earth with non-human beings (Sobion & Willenswaard, 2023). The economics of Pope Francis can give us hope in this endeavor.

References

Bateson, G. (1972). *Steps to an ecology of mind: Collected essays in anthropology, psychiatry, evolution, and epistemology*. The University of Chicago Press.

Bateson, G. (1979). *Mind and nature: A necessary unity*. Hampton Press.

BEC. (2023). https://www.businessethicscenter.com/the-economy-of-francesco-workshop/. Accessed December 9, 2025.

Bouckaert, L., Opdebeeck, H., & Zsolnai, L. (Eds.). (2008). *Frugality: Rebalancing material and spiritual values in economic life*. Peter Lang Academic Publishing.

Brown, P. G. (2015). Ethics for economics in the anthropocene. In P. G. Brown & P. Timmerman (Eds.), *Ecological economics for the Anthropocene: An emerging paradigm* (pp. 66–88). Columbia University Press.

Bruni, L., & Zamagni, S. (2008). Civil economy. Efficiency, equity, public happiness. *Society and Business Review*, *3*(3), 258–259.

Bruni, L., & Zamagni, S. (2016). *Civil economy: Another idea of the market*. Columbia University Press.

Charlton, N. G. (2008). *Understanding Gregory Bateson. Mind, beauty, and the sacred earth*. SUNY Press.

Daly, H. (1996). *Beyond growth: The economics of sustainable development*. Beacon Press.

Douthwaite, R. (1996). *Short circuit. Strengthening local economics for security in an unstable world*. The Lilliput Press.

EoF (2023). https://francescoeconomy.org/. Accessed December 9, 2025.

Fox, W. (1990). *Toward a transpersonal ecology*. Shambhala Publications.

Francis, P. (2013). *Apostolic exhortation evangelii gaudium of the Holy Father Francis to the Bishops, Clergy, Consecrated Persons, and the Lay Faithful on the proclamation of the Gospel in today's world*. https://www.vatican.va/content/francesco/en/apost_exhortations/documents/papa-francesco_esortazione-ap_20131124_evangelii-gaudium.html. Accessed November 6, 2023.

Francis, P. (2015). *Encyclical letter Laudato si' of the Holy Father Francis on care for our common home*. https://www.vatican.va/content/francesco/en/encyclicals/documents/papa-francesco_20150524_enciclica-laudato-si.html. Accessed November 6, 2023.

Francis, P. (2020). *Encyclical letter Fratelli Tutti of the Holy Farther Francis on fraternity and social friendship*. https://www.vatican.va/content/francesco/en/encyclicals/documents/papa-francesco_20201003_enciclica-fratelli-tutti.html. Accessed March 24, 2024.

Georgescu-Roegen, N. (1971). *The entropy law and the economic process*. Harvard University Press.

Global Footprint Network. (2023). https://www.footprintnetwork.org/. Accessed March 12, 2023.

Gowdy, J. (1997). *Limited wants, unlimited means. A reader on hunter-gatherer economics and the environment*. Island Press.

O'Higgins, E., & Zsolnai, L. (Eds.). (2017). *Progressive business models: Creating sustainable and pro-social enterprise*. Palgrave-Macmillan.

Shrivastava, P., & Zsolnai, L. (2022). Wellbeing-oriented organizations: Connecting human flourishing with ecological regeneration. *Business Ethics, the Environment, and Responsibility*, *31*(2), 386–397.

Sobion, J., & van Willenswaard, H. (Eds.). (2023). *Reflections on Earth trusteeship. Mother Earth and a new 21st-century governance paradigm*. Right Livelihood College.

Tornielli, A., & Galeazzi, G. (2015). *This economy kills: Pope Francis on capitalism and social justice*. Liturgical Press.

Veress, T. (2023). Principles and models of community economies. In L. Zsolnai, T. Walker, & P. Shrivastava (Eds.), *Value creation for a sustainable world: Innovating for ecological regeneration and human flourishing* (pp. 239–262). Palgrave-Macmillan.

Zsolnai, L. (2002). Green business or community economy? *International Journal of Social Economics*, *29*(8), 652–662.

Zsolnai, L. (2011). Environmental ethics for business sustainability. *International Journal of Social Economics*, *38*(11), 892–899.

Zsolnai, L. (2017). Frugality and the intrinsic value of nature. In O. Jakobsen & L. Zsolnai (Eds.), *Integral ecology and sustainable business* (pp. 67–76). Emerald.

Zsolnai, L. (2018). Franciscan spirituality and economics. *Religions*, *9*(10), 288. https://doi.org/10.3390/rel9100288. Acessed December 9, 2025.

Zsolnai, L. (2021). Business and Violence. In M. Chatterji & P. Gangopadhyay (Eds.), *New frontiers in conflict management and peace economics: With a focus on human security* pp. 133–140. Emerald Publishing.

Zsolnai, L., Walker, T., & Shrivastava, P. (Eds.). (2023). *Value creation for a sustainable world: Innovating for ecological regeneration and human flourishing*. Palgrave-Macmillan.

Chapter 4
Buddhist Economics

Early Buddhism was primarily a monastic spiritual tradition that focused on personal inner development as a means of alleviating suffering and achieving enlightenment (Harvey, 2013). Nevertheless, Payutto (1994) asserts that the Buddha delivered several teachings on economic matters. He argues that providing people with basic necessities is one of the most important tasks from an economic point of view and emphasizes that Buddhist teachings do not prohibit the accumulation of wealth for laypeople, if it is generated and used in an ethical manner. Regarding wealth, it is praiseworthy to practice contentment for one's own benefit and practice generosity for the benefit of others, but being greedy should be avoided.

Buddhist philosophy is not substantivist but fundamentally relational. There is no eternal "God" in Buddhism, but it presupposes that every being has Buddha-nature, which refers to the capacity for enlightenment and freedom, as well as a fundamental core of goodness, wisdom, and compassion (Encyclopedia of Buddhism, 2023).

Buddhist meditation practices lead to the insight that a stable, unchanging self does not exist. Based on experiences with meditation, the ontological basis of early Buddhism was thus the teaching of "no-self," but later, with Mahayana Buddhism, the emphasis shifted from no-self to the interconnectedness and interdependence of things (Rahula, 1974). Nevertheless, no-self (Puntasen, 2007; Zsolnai, 2007) and interconnectedness (Inoue, 1997; Nelson, 2006; Brown, 2017) play a central role in the Buddhist approach to economics and management.

This chapter uses materials from the author's previously published papers: "Buddhism and Economic Development" In: Todd Lewis, and Gary DeAngelis (Eds.): *Teaching Buddhism*. 2016. Oxford, Oxford University Press. pp. 344–360., "Western Economics versus Buddhist Economics" *Society and Economy*, 29(2): 145–153. https://doi.org/10.1556/socec.29.2007.2.2 and "Buddhist Economics: An Overview" *Society and Economy* 40(4): 497–513. https://doi.org/10.1556/204.2018.40.4.2. Permissions are given by the Publishers.

© The Author(s), under exclusive license to Springer Nature Switzerland AG 2026
L. Zsolnai, *Planet Positive Economy*, Springer Studies in Alternative Economics,
https://doi.org/10.1007/978-3-032-21131-6_4

4.1 Buddhist Economics in the Making

The discourse on Buddhist Economics begins with British economist E. F. Schumacher. In the 1950s and 1960s, Schumacher was working as an economic advisor in South-East Asia, including Burma. He realized that western economic models are not appropriate for Buddhist countries because they are based on a different metaphysics than Far Eastern worldviews.

In his best-selling book *Small is beautiful*, Schumacher (1973) states that the central values of Buddhist economics are simplicity and nonviolence. From a Buddhist point of view, the optimal pattern of consumption involves achieving a high level of human satisfaction through a low rate of material consumption. This will allow people to live without pressure and strain and to fulfill the primary injunction of Buddhism: "Cease to do evil; try to do good." As natural resources are limited everywhere, people living simple lifestyles are obviously less likely to be at each other's throats than those overly dependent on scarce natural resources.

According to Buddhists, engaging in production using local resources to meet local needs is the most rational way of organizing economic life. Dependence on imports from afar and the consequent need for export production are uneconomic and justifiable only in exceptional cases. For Buddhists, there is an essential difference between renewable and nonrenewable resources. Nonrenewable resources must be used only if they are absolutely indispensable, and then only with the greatest care and concern for conservation. Using nonrenewable resources heedlessly or extravagantly is an act of violence. Economizing should be based on renewable resources as much as possible (Schumacher, 1973).

Schumacher (1973) concludes that the Buddhist approach to economics represents a middle way between the modern growth-based economy and traditional stagnation. It seeks the appropriate path of development, the "Right Livelihood" for people.

Schumacher's conception of Buddhist Economics became popular in the west from the 1970s onward, especially among members of alternative and environmental movements. It was gradually recognized that Buddhist economics is not only relevant to Buddhist countries but can also help western countries solve their own problems, namely, overconsumption, welfare malaise, and the destruction of nature.

One seminal contribution to Buddhist economics from Asia was made by the Thai Buddhist monk and philosopher Payutto (1994) in his book *A Middle Way for the Market Place*. He emphasizes that Buddhist teaching recognizes two different kinds of wanting: (1) *tanha*, the desire for objects of pleasure; and (2) *chanda*, the desire for well-being. Tanha is based on ignorance, while chanda is based on wisdom. For example, people who are driven by taṇhā may seek to satisfy the blind craving for sensual pleasure, which may involve a desire for pleasant tastes. But when guided by chanda, desires are directed to realizing well-being.

Payutto (1994) stresses that from the Buddhist point of view, economic activity should be a means to a good and noble life. Production, consumption, and other economic activities are not ends in themselves; they are means, and the end to which they must lead is the development of the well-being of the individual, society, and the environment. Given that there are two kinds of desire, chanda and taṇhā, Payutto argues that there are two kinds of value, which we might term "true value" and "artificial value." True value is created by Chanda. In other words, a commodity's true value is determined by its ability to meet the need for well-being. Conversely, artificial value is created by taṇhā—a commodity's capacity to satisfy the desire for pleasure. Consequently, we can distinguish between two kinds of consumption: "right" consumption and "wrong" consumption. Right consumption based on chanda is the use of goods and services to achieve true well-being. Wrong consumption arises from taṇhā; it is the use of goods and services to satisfy the desire for pleasing sensations or ego-gratification.

Central to Buddhist doctrine is the wisdom of moderation. According to the Buddhist approach, economic activity must be grounded in the goal of achieving well-being rather than "maximum satisfaction." In the mainstream western economic model, unlimited desires may be controlled by economic scarcity, but in the Buddhist ideal model, they are controlled by an appreciation of moderation and the objective of raising well-being.

Payutto (1994) suggests that nonconsumption can also contribute to well-being. Though monks eat only two meals a day before noon, they strive for a kind of well-being that is dependent on minimal inputs. However, if abstinence did not lead to well-being, it would be pointless—little more than a way of mistreating monastics. The question is not whether to consume, but whether our choices lead to self-development.

Production is always accompanied by destruction. In some cases, the destruction is acceptable; in others, it is not. Production is only truly justified when the value of the thing produced outweighs the value of that which is destroyed. In some cases, it is better to refrain from production. In industries where production entails the destruction of natural resources and environmental degradation, nonproduction is sometimes the better choice. Seen in this light, nonproduction can be a useful "activity." A person who produces little in material terms may, at the same time, consume much less of the world's resources and lead a life that benefits the world around them. Such a person is of more value than one who diligently consumes large amounts of the world's resources while manufacturing goods that are harmful to society (Payutto, 1994).

Payutto (1994) summarizes the basic aims of Buddhist economics as follows: (1) the realization of true well-being, and (2) not harming oneself or others. The Middle Way, the right amount, and knowing moderation may be considered synonyms for balance or equilibrium. Knowing moderation means knowing the optimum amount—how much is "just enough and right." This optimum point (or point of balance) is attained when one experiences satisfaction at having responded to the need for quality of life or well-being. From a Buddhist perspective, economic activities are related to the three interconnected aspects of human existence: human beings, society, and the natural environment. Economic activities must take place in a way that does not harm oneself (by reducing quality of life) or others (by causing problems in society or the environment).

In his book *Putting Buddhism to Work*, former Japanese banker and economic thinker Inoue (1997) presented his view of economics and Buddhism. Inoue claims that the Buddhist motivation for work must be the pursuit of the interests of both oneself and others. According to Inoue, Buddhist economic activities do not have profit as the principal goal. Instead, their primary objective is to serve the community in a wider sense. Profit may come, but it is a by-product rather than the main goal of business activities.

Inoue (1997) emphasizes that living necessarily involves the taking of the lives of other beings. We cannot change that, but we can limit how many lives we take and to what extent we allow our desires to be satisfied. Gratitude toward other beings and a sense of regret about harming others are crucial elements of Buddhism. This calls for the environmental and social assessment of products and industries, which is already a highly developed practice in Japan and other advanced countries.

Inoue (1997) suggests that both production (P) and consumption (C) should be assessed. Production can be ranked according to four levels:

P1 = production that has a negligible negative impact on the environment,
P2 = production that has a minimal negative impact on the environment,
P3 = production that has some negative impact on the environment,
P4 = production that involves a great deal of negative impact on the environment.

Consumption can also be assessed using a four-item ranking system:

C1 = consumption of goods that are vital for human existence,
C2 = consumption of goods that are not absolutely necessary, but make living better,
C3 = consumption of goods that are not very necessary,
C4 = consumption of goods that are frivolous or even harmful.

The combination of these variables is used to determine whether the manufacture of a product is relatively earth-friendly and whether its consumption is truly necessary. The lower the combined number, the better the product is for the environment and society. From a Buddhist perspective, all economic enterprises must be understood in the context of the entire natural universe, so that ignoring environmental and social costs is unacceptable. Economic efficiency should be redefined as "not wasting." For example, although recycling takes time and money, and may seem inefficient and troublesome, ultimately, we are more efficient when we recycle and do not waste products. Accordingly, recycling culture is economically sound (Inoue, 1997).

In his publications, Thai economist Apichai Puntasen addresses macroeconomic problems from an ideal Buddhist perspective (Puntasen, 2005, 2007). Because of the different meanings of "happiness," Puntasen suggests using the word *sukha*, which is drawn from the teaching of the Buddha. One meaning of sukha is "wellness." Sukha also implies a state where pain is reduced from its original level. Less pain implies more sukha. On the other hand, pleasure does not necessarily imply less pain.

Sukha derived from acquisition is considered a lower level of sukha. It may be thought of as hedonism in the western sense. However, achieving this form of sukha must not impose any burden on oneself or any other living beings. Even with this qualification, Buddhism recommends the attainment of a higher level of sukha, which arises from nonacquisition, although it can also be derived from giving or helping others relieve their pain. The highest levels of sukha are derived from meditation, with the highest of all being associated with being emancipated or liberated from all impurities of mind or all defilements: i.e., *nirvāṇa* (Puntasen, 2005, 2007).

It can be seen that sukha is more strongly associated with mental development than with any form of material acquisition. The most important method for achieving this mental state is training the mind through meditation to reach the stage of *panna* (Sanskrit: *prajna*; i.e., wisdom or insight), the ability to understand reality clearly, and everything according to its own nature. Therefore, paññā is instrumental in obtaining relief from suffering. With no suffering, sukha or wellness of the mind may prevail, despite the inevitable decline of the mortal body. An individual who has perfected one's paññā may experience enlightenment. Puntasen (2005, 2007) thus suggests that the mode of production in Buddhist economics can be defined as paññā-ism. Human beings who have paññā center their lives around compassion and act dispassionately; they do not seek to maximize pleasure or utility but endeavor to relieve others of suffering as much as possible.

According to Puntasen (2005, 2007), paññā can be used to examine the factors of economic input, such as technology, forms of capital, and natural resources. Production processes should enhance the good qualities associated with human inputs. The process should generate human skills and creativity as well as provide a sense of fulfillment at the workplace. The use of non-renewable resources should be constantly minimized, while the use of renewable resources should be encouraged as much as possible. Waste from production processes should be kept to a minimum. The need to increase production to meet rising demand for consumption is not required in Buddhist economics, since consumption should also be moderated. As only moderate consumption is needed, any surplus products can be donated to others who are still in need. Peace and tranquility result from the ability to understand everything in terms of its own nature, or having paññā.

4.2 Principles of Buddhist Economics

The five principles of Buddhist economics constitute a strategy of minimization—namely, (1) minimizing suffering, (2) simplifying desires, (3) practicing nonviolence, (4) genuine care, and (5) generosity (Zsolnai, 2008). The Buddhist economic strategy is in opposition to the western strategy of maximization and can be implemented in practice in any economic setting (Zsolnai, 2007) and in Buddhist and non-Buddhist countries alike (Brown & Zsolnai, 2018).

The underlying principle of Buddhist economics is to minimize the suffering of all sentient beings, including nonhuman beings. From a Buddhist viewpoint, a project is worthy of being undertaken if it reduces the suffering of those affected. The suffering-minimizing principle can be formulated as the claim that the goal of economic activities is not to produce gains but to reduce losses. Since humans (and other sentient beings) display loss sensitivity (Tversky & Kahneman, 1991, 1992), it is worth trying to reduce losses to oneself and others rather than trying to increase gains for them. Losses should not be interpreted only in monetary terms or applied only to humans. The capability of experiencing losses, i.e., suffering, is universal in both human and nonhuman realms.

Buddhist economics suggests not multiplying but *simplifying human desires*. Above the minimum level of material comfort, which includes enough food, clothing, shelter, and medicine, it is wise to reduce one's desires. Wanting less may bring substantial benefits to the person, community, and nature as a whole. Buddhism recommends moderate consumption and directly aims at changing one's preferences through meditation, reflection, analysis, autosuggestion, and the like. Payutto (1994) identifies the goal of Buddhist economics based on the distinction of taṇhā and chanda: the realization of true well-being, in which the practice of aspiration (chanda) plays a central role. True well-being means satisfying basic needs through optimal economic means and reducing desires by cultivating simplicity (Payutto, 1994). In other words, Buddhist economics aims to create shared prosperity in a sustainable world with less suffering (Brown & Zsolnai, 2018).

Nonviolence (*ahimsa*) is the main guiding value of Buddhist economics in terms of solving social problems. Acts should not cause harm to the doer or the receiver. Practicing nonviolence means refraining from engaging in actions that directly cause suffering to oneself or others and engaging in finding participative and communicative solutions. Community economy models, in which communities of producers and consumers are formed to meet both their needs at the lowest cost and with reduced risk through long-term arrangements, are good examples of this. The community economy uses local resources to meet the needs of local people rather than the wants of markets far away. The community economy is based on partial or complete self-reliance (Douthwaite, 1996).

Buddhist economics favors practicing genuine care. Cornell University economist Robert Frank (2004) differentiated five distinct cases in which socially responsible organizations are rewarded for the higher cost of caring. (1) Opportunistic behavior can be avoided between owners and managers. (2) Getting moral satisfaction, employees are ready to work more for lower salaries. (3) High-quality new employees can be recruited. (4) Customer loyalty can be gained. (5) The trust of subcontractors can be established. Caring organizations are rewarded for the higher costs of their socially responsible behavior by their ability to build and sustain commitment among owners, managers, and employees and to establish trusting relationships with customers and subcontractors.

Buddhist economics suggests that generosity might work in business and social life because people behave like *Homo Reciprocans*—they tend to reciprocate what they get, and they often give back more than they receive. Homo Reciprocans enter new social situations with a propensity to cooperate and share, respond to cooperative behavior by maintaining or increasing their level of cooperation, and respond to selfish, free-riding behavior by retaliating against offenders, even at a cost to themselves and even when they cannot reasonably expect future personal gains from such retaliation (Bowles et al., 1997).

The contrast between mainstream Western economics and Buddhist economics can be illustrated as two frameworks in opposition (Zsolnai, 2007). Mainstream western economics represents a maximizing framework. It is designed to maximize profits, desires, markets, instrumental use, and self-interest, and tends to build a world where "bigger is better" and "more is more." Buddhist economics represents a minimizing framework where suffering, desires, violence, instrumental use, and self-interest should be minimized. This is why "small is beautiful" and "less is more" nicely express the essence of the Buddhist approach to economic questions.

In Buddhism, "Buddha-nature" is the basic, non-negotiable value assumption. It implies no-self, from which the values of simplicity, compassion for all beings, and nonviolence are derived. These values together induce well-being as a superordinate value of Buddhism.

Buddhism involves taking a nonanthropocentric worldview and a noninstrumental approach to life and existence. The ultimate goal of a Buddhist life is liberation, which can be attained through selfless, compassionate care for other beings.

4.3 Buddhist Economic Working Models

Patagonia

Patagonia, Inc. is a California-based company established by Buddhist practitioner Yvon Chouinard. It produces outdoor clothing products and equipment. In the early

2020s, the company employed approximately 2000 people across more than 50 countries on five continents, generating over USD 1 billion in sales (Patagonia, 2023).

Patagonia aims to produce the best outdoor products without harming nature unnecessarily. Its effects on the natural environment are made fully transparent and are sufficiently reduced and neutralized throughout its supply chain. Patagonia is involved in raising consumer consciousness, increasing product durability, reducing its carbon footprint, supporting environmental movements and campaigns, and promoting business transformation by supporting businesses with similar commitments (Patagonia, 2023).

Due to Chouinard's spiritual commitment, derived from Zen Buddhism and a nature-respecting mountaineering culture, environmental and social sustainability have always been central to Patagonia. The core values of the company are related to the interconnectedness of nature and all sentient beings, harmony, responsibility, cooperation, and the internal development and self-realization of stakeholders. To fulfill its purpose, Patagonia has bought up large areas of wild nature in Patagonia, Chile, to preserve them for future generations (Chouinard, 2006; Patagonia, 2023).

In September 2022, Yvon Chouinard donated his company entirely "to the Earth." He proclaimed that "Earth is now our only shareholder" (Ims & Zsolnai, 2022). Instead of extracting value from nature and transforming it into wealth for investors, the wealth Patagonia creates is entirely used to protect the Earth. One hundred percent of the company's voting stock was transferred to the Patagonia Purpose Trust, created to sustain the company's values, and 100% of the nonvoting stock was given to the Holdfast Collective, a nonprofit organization dedicated to fighting the environmental crisis and defending nature (Patagonia, 2023).

Greyston Bakery

Greyston Bakery is a for-profit social enterprise founded in 1982 by Zen Buddhist leader Bernard Glassman in New York. The company is famous for producing high-quality baked goods and ice cream products. It practices an "open hiring" policy, which means anyone can apply to work with them, regardless of their background, including people with a criminal record. Besides the bakery, Greyston also has a foundation comprising an integrated network of not-for-profit and for-profit entities that provide jobs, workforce development, affordable housing, community gardens, youth services, childcare, and healthcare to the local community. Greyston aims to be a force for self-transformation and community economic renewal (Greyston Bakery, 2023).

Greyston is a successful social enterprise with a spiritually rooted philosophy that fuels community development and commitment to spiritual growth. The founder's main inspiration was establishing a business that could reduce human suffering. Greyston's business model is based on key Buddhist concepts: the mandala (wholeness) and the path (transformation). According to these concepts, the company is managed in the belief that everything is interconnected and that one cannot afford to ignore sectors of society. Greyston places great emphasis on personal empowerment and transformation. Employees are encouraged to develop a sense of responsibility for themselves, their families, and their co-workers. Gainful employment is seen as the first step on an individual's path toward success. Social justice, economic development, and personal empowerment are the most important building blocks that support the operations of Greyston as a company (Zsolnai, 2015).

Apopo

Apopo is a Belgian social enterprise that works in Tanzania, Mozambique, Thailand, Angola, and Cambodia. It researches, develops, and implements rat-detection technologies for humanitarian purposes, such as identifying landmines and tuberculosis (Apopo, 2023).

In 1995, Apopo was founded by a Zen Buddhist monk and social activist, Bart Weetjens, he was exploring solutions to the global problem of landmines. He found that rats—intelligent, cheap, and widespread throughout the world—are able to detect the scent of mines and even tuberculosis. Among the core values of Apopo are quality, innovation, diversity, and social transformation, including developing skills, creating jobs, improving socioeconomic and environmental conditions, freeing up land for development, and combating public health issues (Zsolnai, 2015).

Loden Entrepreneurs

In 1999, Buddhist scholar and social activist Karma Phuntsho established the Loden Foundation in Bhutan. The foundation supports Bhutanese self-made entrepreneurs. Loden entrepreneurs run small-scale, locally based enterprises that integrate spiritual values into their business operations, thereby laying the foundation for committed, innovative, and ethical business behavior in the country. Loden entrepreneurs follow Buddhist spiritual and ethical values and are called "Bodhisattva entrepreneurs" (Loden Foundation, 2024).

Table 4.1 presents the visions, means, and outcomes of the selected Buddhist economic and business models.

Table 4.1 Main characteristics of selected buddhist business organizations and economic initiatives

	Vision	Means	Outcomes
Patagonia	Produce high-quality outdoor clothes and apparel, and use business to protect and restore natural ecosystems	Minimalist style, simplicity, transparency, innovation in the retailing of ecological outdoor clothing and apparel aimed at developing consumer consciousness and supporting the environmental movement "Our only shareholder is the Earth."	Monitoring and reducing the company's carbon footprint, participating in regenerative agriculture, buying large areas of wild nature, and donating all future profits to saving the Earth
Greyston Bakery	Practice of interconnectedness and personal transformation	Producing high-quality brownies and cookies, implementing an open-hire policy, and investing in community renewal projects	Fair and lasting relationships with homeless and disadvantaged employees, providing jobs and other opportunities for them
Apopo	Effective, humanitarian help for people in Africa and Asia whose lives are threatened by war and disease	Using trained rats to detect landmines and tuberculosis	Thousands of lives saved, socioeconomic and health development programs, and the transformation of the perception of rats among the general public
Loden Foundation	Establishing Bodhisattva entrepreneurship	Train and support small-scale, local entrepreneurs to initiate business projects that support the renewal of Bhutan's economy while preserving local culture and the natural environment	Dozens of new business ventures that bring innovative and ethical business practices to the country

Source Author's construction

4.4 Summary

The important question is whether Buddhist economics can penetrate the modern economy to prevent it from driving us along a materially unsustainable path and uproot its growing hold on our psychological state (Zadek, 1997).

Buddhist economics is best viewed as an alternative strategy that can be applied across a variety of economic contexts. Buddhist economics may help Buddhists and non-Buddhists alike create sustainable livelihood solutions that aim to reduce the suffering of human and nonhuman beings by practicing want-negation, nonviolence, caring, and generosity.

References

Apopo. (2023). https://apopo.org/?v=35b528213b8. Accessed July 6, 2023.

Bowles, S., Boyd, R., Fehr, E., & Gintis, H. (1997, June 7). *Homo reciprocans: A research initiative on the origins, dimensions, and policy implications of reciprocal fairness*. Santa Fe Research Initiative on Reciprocal Fairness.

Brown, C. (2017). *Buddhist economics: An enlightened approach to the dismal science*. Bloomsbury Press.

Brown, C., & Zsolnai, L. (2018). Buddhist economics: An overview. *Society and Economy*, *40*(4), 497–513.

Chouinard, Y. (2006). *Let My People Go Surfing: The Education of a Reluctant Businessman*. Penguin Books.

Douthwaite, R. (1996). *Short circuit. Strengthening local economics for security in an unstable World*. The Lilliput Press.

Encyclopedia of Buddhism. (2023). https://encyclopediaofbuddhism.org/wiki/Buddha-nature. Accessed August 19, 2023.

Foundation, L. (2024). https://www.loden.org/. Accessed December 18, 2024.

Frank, R. (2004). Can socially responsible firms survive in competitive environments? In *R. Frank: What price the moral high ground? Ethical dilemmas in competitive environments*. Princeton University Press.

Greyston Bakery. (2023). https://shop.greyston.org/. Accessed July 6, 2023.

Harvey, P. (2013). *An introduction to Buddhism. Teachings, history, and practices*. Cambridge University Press.

Ims, K., & Zsolnai, L. (2022). Earth is our only shareholder—Yvon Chouinard, Patagonia. https://magazine.omrise.org/2022/12/earth-is-our-only-shareholder-yvon-chouinard-patagonia/. Accessed July 6, 2023.

Inoue, S. (1997). *Putting Buddhism to work*. Kodansha International Ltd.

Nelson, J. A. (2006). The relational firm: A Buddhist and Feminist analysis. In L. Zsolnai & K. J. Ims (Eds.), *Business within limits. Deep ecology and Buddhist economics* (pp. 195–219). Peter Lang Academic Publisher.

Patagonia. (2023). https://www.patagonia.com/home/. Accessed July 6, 2023.

Payutto, P. A. (1994). *Buddhist economics: A middle way for the market place*. Buddhadhamma Foundation.

Puntasen, A. (2005). *Buddhist economics: Evolution, theories and its application to various economic subjects*. Amarin Publisher.

Puntasen, A. (2007). Buddhist economics as a new paradigm towards happiness. *Society and Economy*, *29*(2), 181–200.

Rahula, W. (1974). *What the Buddha taught*. Grove Press.

Schumacher, E. F. (1973). *Small is beautiful. Economics as if people mattered*. Abacus.

Tversky, A., & Kahneman, D. (1991). Loss Aversion in riskless choice: A reference-dependent model. *Quarterly Journal of Economics*, *106*(4), 1039–1061.

Tversky, A., & Kahneman, D. (1992). Advances in prospect theory: Cumulative representation of uncertainty. *Journal of Risk and Uncertainty*, *5*, 297–323.

Zadek, S. (1997). Towards a progressive Buddhist economics. In J. Watts, A. Senauke, & S. Bhikku (Eds.), *Entering the realm of reality: Towards dharmic societies* (pp. 241–273). INEB.

Zsolnai, L. (2007). Western economics versus Buddhist economics. *Society and Economy*, *29*(2), 145–153.

Zsolnai, L. (2008). Buddhist economic strategy. In L. Bouckaert, H. Opdebeeck, & L. Zsolnai (Eds.), *Frugality: Rebalancing material and spiritual values in economic life* (pp. 279–303). Peter Lang Academic Publishers.

Zsolnai, L. (2015). *Post-materialistic business: Spiritual value-orientation in renewing management*. Palgrave–Macmillan.

Chapter 5
Lessons from Hindu Spirituality

This chapter is written to show how Hindu spirituality can be used in management today. It presents S. K. Chakraborty's attempts to bring Hindu spirituality into management, drawing on insights from Vedanta philosophy and its modern proponents, such as Rabindranath Tagore, Swami Vivekananda, Mahatma Gandhi, and Sri Aurobindo. Finally, the case of Aravind Eye Care System is discussed to illustrate how Hindu spirituality can catalyze the development of alternative ways of thinking and acting toward a safe and sane future.

5.1 Hindu Spirituality

Hindu spirituality is one of the oldest spiritual traditions known to humanity. *Vedanta* is one of the six orthodox Indian religious-philosophical schools. It is the Hindu philosophy "par excellence" for most Hindus. The term "Vedanta" originally referred to the *Upanishads*, but the *Brahma Sutras* and the *Bhagavad Gita* are also considered its main textual sources. Vedanta is mostly concerned with the questions of *Atman* (the soul) and *Brahman* (the Absolute), and their mystical identification. It has many sub-schools of which *Advaita Vedanta* is the most important one (Chatterji & Zsolnai, 2016).

Advaita Vedanta is mainly based on Adi Shankara's (eighth century AD) commentaries on the principal *Upanishads*, the *Brahma Sutras*, and the *Bhagavad Gita*. According to it, Brahman is the only reality, and the world as it appears to us is illusory. Advaita refers to the nonduality of Atman and Brahman, and liberation takes place when one acquires and realizes this (Chatterji & Zsolnai, 2016).

© The Author(s), under exclusive license to Springer Nature Switzerland AG 2026

L. Zsolnai, *Planet Positive Economy*, Springer Studies in Alternative Economics,
https://doi.org/10.1007/978-3-032-21131-6_5

5.2 Bringing Hindu Spirituality Into Management

Bringing Hindu spirituality into management is championed by S. K. Chakraborty, the Founder of the Management Center for Human Values at the Indian Institute of Management, Calcutta (Fig. 5.1).

Addressing the clash between globalized, market-driven business forces and Indian spiritual values and ethics rooted in Vedanta was the leitmotif of Chakraborty's decades-long endeavor, carried out with inspiration and zeal, to establish and promote an Indian model of management built on India's indigenous knowledge. His seminal contribution has been to anchor a solid spiritual foundation in human values and leadership, drawing on insights from Indian spirituality and its modern proponents such as Rabindranath Tagore, Swami Vivekananda, Mahatma Gandhi, and Sri Aurobindo (Chakraborty, 1997; Chakraborty & Chakraborty, 2008; Mukherjee & Zsolnai, 2022).

Rabindranath Tagore (1861–1941) was a poet, philosopher, and a profound connoisseur of Indian classical writings, epics, and the *Upanishads*. In his works, he conveyed the profound metaphysical teachings rooted in the Vedic tradition. According to him, religion is the essence of human existence, the expression of man's inner nature. Tagore opposed religious fanaticism, asceticism, and dogmatism, and claimed that there was no conflict between science and religion. He emphasized the importance of education and founded schools based on the Vedic traditions, including Visva-Bharati University (Bharati, 2025).

Swami Vivekananda (1864–1902) was one of the first to convey the teachings of Vedanta philosophy and the practical instructions of Yoga to the Western world. He attempted to reconcile Hindu spirituality with the Western material worldview.

Fig. 5.1 S. K. Chakraborty (1940–2018). *Source* Photo by the Author taken in 2001

He preached the essential unity of all religions, emphasizing that different religions lead to the same goal, even if by different paths. He advocated the universal, humanistic side of the *Vedas*, emphasizing that service to humanity is also service to God. He fought against poverty in India and the caste system. He underlined the importance of educating young people and warned against the injustice of gender discrimination, since the soul has neither gender nor caste.

M. K. Gandhi (1869–1948) employed nonviolent civil disobedience and led India to independence. He inspired movements for civil rights and freedom across the world. He did not value nature because it was useful to man, but because it was the creation of God and hence should remain in as pristine a state as possible. For Gandhi, everything that exists in the universe is part of a common omnipresent and omnipotent *Paramatman* and therefore has rights of its own. Gandhi consequently called for limiting wants to minimize humanity's stress on nature.

For Gandhi, the ultimate goal is the attainment of *Moksha*, i.e., freedom from all ills and merging with nature. According to him, it is the universal self, the Atman, that must be realized. Gandhi believed in the concept of *Advaita* (non-duality), which means that the world is one and there is no division between humanity and nature. He recognized a basic, shared right to live and blossom. Our needs will be satisfied if we desire to possess less and are less greedy. He argued that nature produces enough for everyone if everybody takes enough, but no more. Gandhi also believed that all living beings have an equal right to exist on this planet (Kumaria, 2003).

Sri Aurobindo (1872–1950) taught that behind the phenomena of the universe lies the Reality of the Self, which is one and eternal. He promoted the possibility of the evolution of consciousness to people and specified yoga as a means of achieving this. According to him, it is through the development of consciousness that humanity can find inner, direct knowledge and experience. The goal of his yoga practice is the inner self-development of the individual, through which they can discover the One Self present in everything and reach a higher spiritual consciousness that makes human nature divine.

Indian spirituality in management aims to introduce India's indigenous concepts into professional Indian management. In promoting this, Chakraborty published dozens of books on values, ethics, and leadership; he founded three journals and two institutions; and he inspired many business students in India and abroad, as well as thousands of corporate executives and professionals who have gone through his management development programs. Of special mention is the *Journal of Human Values*, of which Chakraborty was the Founder and Editor-in-Chief, published by Sage Publications.

Chakraborty's effort to root business ethics in the traditions of Indian spirituality, particularly in the Vedantic heritage, is challenging for Western ethicists who usually think in terms of theories of rights, the social contract, and utility maximization. Introducing spirituality into the field of business and managerial ethics shifts the focus from external rule-directed behavior toward an inner-directed, existential search for meaning. What is missing in conventional business and managerial ethics is a deep, intersubjective intuition of the presence of life that guides thoughts and actions. Chakraborty calls such an ethic, based on reconnection with the inner source of life, "consciousness ethics," which he rightly distinguishes from compliance ethics and cognitive ethics.

This new focus has not only led to far broader concepts of purpose and success than are traditionally associated with management. It has also given rise to deeper existential questions about the identity and responsibility of corporations and their leaders—questions very similar to those faced by persons on a spiritual quest (Pruzan, 2009; Mukherjee, 2022).

Chakraborty emphasized that the mainstream materialistic value orientation of today's business can hardly be reconciled with any form of genuine spirituality. The dominant understanding of economic rationality—namely, individualistic, self-interest maximization—should be replaced with a broader notion of reason. Nobel Prize-winning economist Sen (2004) suggested that rationality requires subjecting one's choice of action, including objectives, values, and priorities, to reasoned scrutiny. In this way, spiritually inspired choices may not be incompatible with the demands of human reason. Business actors can rationally pursue their objectives based on spiritual values and priorities.

5.3 Aravind Eye Care System

An illustrative case of embedding Hindu spirituality into management is the Aravind Eye Care System. In 1976, inspired by Hindu spirituality, ophthalmologist Dr. Govindappa Venkataswamy, in his endeavor to eliminate avoidable blindness, established an alternative health care model that could supplement government efforts and be self-supporting. Today, the Aravind group of eye hospitals, which he founded, performs 450,000 eye surgeries and procedures each year, making it the largest eye care provider in the world. Since its inception, Aravind has handled more than 65 million outpatient visits and performed more than 7.8 million surgeries (Rattanani, 2025). The Aravind Eye Care System now serves as a model for India and the rest of the world (Aravind Eye Care System, 2024).

5.4 Summary

Hindu spirituality in management can serve as a source of inspiration for academics, business leaders, and management professionals to rethink their roles and responsibilities in transforming business into a more human and ecological enterprise. Upholding and pursuing Hindu spirituality can catalyze the development of alternative ways of thinking and living that lead to a safe, sane, and sustainable future for the self, the organization, the community, society, nations, and the planet at large.

References

Aravind Eye Care System. (2024). https://aravind.org/. Accessed February 17, 2025.

Bharati, V. (2025). https://www.visvabharati.ac.in/. Accessed February 17, 2025.

Chakraborty, S. K. (1997). *Ethics in management: Vedantic perspectives*. Oxford University Press.

Chakraborty, S. K., & Chakraborty, D. (2008). *Spirituality in management: Means or end?* Oxford University Press.

Chatterji, M., & Zsolnai, L. (Eds.). (2016). *Ethical leadership. Indian and European spiritual approaches*. Palgrave-Macmillan.

Kumaria, P. (2003). Nature and man: Gandhian concept of deep ecology. *Anasakti*, *2*, 2003. https://www.gandhiashramsevagram.org/gandhi-articles/nature-and-man-gandhian-concept-of-deep-ecology.php. Accessed December 9, 2025.

Mukherjee, S. (2022). *Looking East. Indian wisdom for modern management*. Peter Lang Academic Publishers.

Mukherjee, S., & Zsolnai, L. (Eds.). (2022). *Global perspectives on Indian spirituality and management. The legacy of S. K. Chakraborty*. Springer.

Pruzan, P. (2009). *Rational, ethical and spiritual perspectives on leadership*. Peter Lang Academic Publishers.

Rattanani, J. (2025). Exploring Gandhian Trusteeship for the age of the Anthropocene. In L. Zsolnai (Ed.), *Spirituality and business in the Anthropocene. Insights from Hinduism, Christianity, Buddhism and existential humanism* (pp. 157–183). Palgrave-Macmillan.

Sen, A. (2004). *Rationality and freedom*. Harvard University Press.

Chapter 6
Indigenous Worldviews

This chapter aims to show how panpsychism and the holism of Indigenous worldviews challenge the materialism and reductionism of modern economics and business. It is emphasized that Indigenous worldviews suggest organizing economic activities in community-based, substantive ways that respect the limits of the natural environment. Seventh Generation, Inc., and Jokkmokk's Market are presented as working models inspired by Indigenous worldviews.

6.1 The Original Affluent Societies

Aboriginal communities have managed to survive for the last 20,000–40,000 years. Their worldviews and economic practices are worthy of study if humanity wants to survive in the Anthropocene.

The concept of *Homo Economicus* does not adequately reflect the economic experiences of humankind: humans lived as hunter-gatherers for about 99% of our entire existence as a species. typically represented "Uneconomic Man," whose wants are limited and who had, exactly for this reason, unlimited means to satisfy their wants. Hunter-gatherer societies were surprisingly abundant and, at the same time, socially equal and environmentally sustainable. For this reason, cultural anthropologists and ecological economists are interested in studying hunter-gatherer economics.

In his classic work *Stone age economics*, cultural anthropologist (Sahlins, 1972) revised traditional views of hunter-gatherers, revealing them as the original "affluent society." He examined notions of production, distribution, and exchange in these early communities and explored the link between economics and cultural and social factors. Hunter-gatherers were able to achieve affluence by balancing means and ends because they wanted little. Sahlins (1972) concluded that the existence of

© The Author(s), under exclusive license to Springer Nature Switzerland AG 2026

L. Zsolnai, *Planet Positive Economy*, Springer Studies in Alternative Economics,
https://doi.org/10.1007/978-3-032-21131-6_6

those living in subsistence economies may have been better, healthier, and more fulfilling than that of the millions who enjoy the affluence and luxury afforded by the economics of modern industrialization and agriculture.

Ecological economist Gowdy (1998) reconstructed the basic features of the hunter-gatherer economic order as follows: (1) the economic notion of "scarcity" is largely a social construct, not an inherent property of human existence; (2) the separation of work from social life is not a necessary characteristic of economic production; (3) the linking of individual wellbeing to individual production is not a necessary characteristic of economic organization; (4) selfishness and acquisitiveness are not natural traits of our species; and (5) inequality based on class and gender is not a necessary characteristic of human society.

In hunter-gatherer societies, work is social and cooperative. It is integrated with ritual, socialization, and artistic expression. The work-leisure trade-off appears to be absent. In many hunter-gatherer societies, there is no formal connection between producers and recipients of economic output. The distribution of goods is based on strikingly different principles from the criterion of marginal productivity favored by modern capitalism (Zsolnai, 1999).

Whereas industrial economies are using the Earth's stock of nonrenewable natural resources, especially fossil fuels, hunter-gatherers lived off the flows of renewable biological resources and used solar energy through their ecosystems. The capital in their world was not a physical thing that could be manipulated and controlled, but took the form of knowledge that could be shared and was accessible to all. This is why private property was virtually unknown to hunter-gatherer societies. Hunter-gatherers were basically, or in many cases even "aggressively," egalitarian. In their societies, power and authority were kept in check (Zsolnai, 1999).

What can we learn from hunter-gatherer economics? Given the current population of Earth, we certainly cannot return to a hunting-and-gathering way of life. However, we can try to incorporate some basic features of the hunter-gatherer societies that worked relatively well in promoting ecological balance and social harmony. These features include social security, living off renewable flows rather than exhaustible stocks, sexual equality, cultural and ecological diversity based on bio-regionalism, and social rather than private property. The real crux of the matter is the question of scale. Hunter-gatherers lived in small-scale communities and used simple, viable technologies. It is not certain that the attractive features of these little societies can be realized in any form in our large-scale, globalized societies. Hunter-gatherer economics can serve only as a heuristic model for our age.

6.2 The Panpsychism of Indigenous Worldviews

Hart (2010) summarizes the main features of Indigenous worldviews as follows. (1) All things exist according to the principle of survival. (2) This energy is part of some grand design. (3) All things have a role to play to ensure balance and harmony and the overall wellbeing of life. (4) All things are an extension of the grand design, and, as such, contain the same essence as the source from which they flow. (5) This essence is understood as "spirit," which links all things to each other and to Creation.

The principles of Indigenous worldviews can be captured as follows. First, knowledge is holistic, cyclical, and dependent on relationships and connections with living and nonliving beings and entities. Second, there are many truths, and these truths depend on individual experiences. Third, everything is alive. Fourth, all things are equal. Fifth, the land is sacred. Sixth, the relationship between people and the spiritual world is important. Seventh, human beings are not considered the most important entities in the world (Hart, 2010).

The famous Australian Aboriginal proverb nicely expresses this philosophy. "We are all visitors to this place. We are just passing through. Our purpose here is to observe, to learn, to grow, to love, . . . , and then we return home."

Indigenous worldviews seem to be at odds with modern Western philosophy and science. However, there is a new wave of thinking that supports the panpsychist position associated with Indigenous worldviews.

Panpsychism is re-emerging today as an approach to social practice. It is based on the assumption that consciousness or mind is a fundamental and ubiquitous feature of reality. This philosophical position is supported by recent discoveries in transpersonal psychology, which show that, under specific circumstances, people can directly experience the subjective side of the existence of non-human beings, living and non-living, small and large.

Norwegian philosopher Arne Johan Vetlesen (2015) says that panpsychism contrasts starkly with market thinking and the materialist position that is dominant in the Western world today. The typical Western individual has developed a kind of autistic behavior vis-à-vis the world that "discourages" him or her "from opening up to and engaging in communicative exchanges with the (non-human) world" (Vetlesen, 2015: 196).

The panpsychist position involves communicative exchange between humans and non-humans, in addition to inter-human exchange, which invites a sort of participation mystique. This is the opposite of disengagement from others and from nature, and of viewing the world as an "object," something "out there" as an external entity. The panpsychist position is a rich framework built on revelatory insights originating from humans as well as nonhuman others (Ims, 2022).

6.3 Working Models Inspired by Indigenous Worldviews

Jeffrey Hollender, an American authority on corporate responsibility, sustainability, and social equity, co-founded Seventh Generation, Inc. in 1988. The company became a leading brand of natural products known for its authenticity, transparency, and progressive business practices.

Seventh Generation articulates a commitment to go beyond producing cleaner and greener products. It wants to create cultural change and shape consumer behavior and business ethics. Living up to its name (taken from the *Great Iroquois Law* that prescribes deliberation of the impact of all of our activities on the next seven generations), the novel formulas of the company's household and personal care products ensure that consumers can make a difference by keeping toxic material out of the environment, preserving natural resources, and reducing pollution (Zsolnai, 2015).

The company's products are manufactured in the most sustainable way possible. The ingredients used in products such as dishwashing liquids, laundry detergents, household cleaners, and feminine care items are safe for the environment and pose no health risks. Paper products are made using only recycled, bleach-free paper (Zsolnai, 2015).

The company's environmental sensitivity is manifested in its product development standards, the materials it uses, product transportation and other emissions-related activities, regulatory compliance, lifecycle analysis, systems thinking, and its use of biomimicry in product and packaging design. The company encourages consumers to get involved in their efforts to save the planet. Green tips, ideas for better products, and reviews of existing products are proactively sought from customers through the company's website. The organization's newsletter helps consumers make informed choices and raises environmental awareness (Zsolnai, 2015).

Seventh Generation exists through its belief in the role of commerce to remake the world and its espousal of a new corporate paradigm that is concerned with more than protecting the environment. It helps develop new markets, position more responsible products and brands in these markets, and attract a vibrant workforce that is committed to making a change. Through its innovative business practices, the company has created avenues for suppliers, partners, shareholders, customers, and employees to express their idealism, passion, and commitment to causes larger than themselves at every point of the value chain—truly making a difference one household cleaning spray at a time (Seventh Generation, 2025).

The Jokkmokk Market is a 400-year-old winter market in Jokkmokk, Northern Sweden. It is based on Sami cultural traditions and uses them to develop sustainable tourism in the region. The Sami culture is the main reason to visit the place, both during the Jokkmokk Winter Market and at other times of the year (Sörensson, 2023).

Jokkmokk is an important village for the Sami, an Indigenous people living in Norway, Sweden, Finland, and Russia. They are mainly known for their fine craftsmanship and reindeer herding. The Sami also speak their own languages. They founded the Winter Market in Jokkmokk, which today is a large event that creates sustainable value not only for the local community but also for the many tourists who visit.

Since 1605, Jokkmokk's three-day Winter Market has been held annually, beginning on the first Thursday in February, which is a very cold time of year (temperatures can dip to −40°C during this period). Attracting tens of thousands of visitors from around the world, the market also remains the foremost meeting place for Sami people across the entire Sápmi region. In addition to personal meet-ups, there are lectures, art exhibitions, handicraft exhibitions, and "Jojk" concerts (Jojk is a style of singing in Sami cultures). The winter market is the most important event for the cultural and creative industries in the Nordic hemisphere and serves as a unique meeting place for the Sami People. A clear trend in Jokkmokk is that small-business owners and entrepreneurs in the growing tourism industry are now settling down and becoming permanent residents. Despite the numerous challenges, reindeer herding remains strong in Jokkmokk, and several projects are underway to develop side branches of the industry (Sörensson, 2023).

The case of the Jokkmokk market shows that it is possible to preserve local Indigenous culture when combined with creative industries and sustainability-oriented tourism.

References

Gowdy, J. (Ed.). (1998). *Limited wants, unlimited means*. Island Press.
Hart, M. A. (2010). Indigenous worldviews, knowledge, and research: The development of an indigenous research paradigm. *Journal of Indigenous Voices in Social Work, 1*(1), 1–16.
Ims, K. J. (2022). *Deep ecology, business ethics and personal responsibility*. Peter Lang Academic Publishers.
Sahlins, M. (1972). *Stone age economics*. Aldin-Atherton, Inc.
Seventh Generations. (2025). https://www.seventhgeneration.com/. Accessed February 18, 2025.
Sörensson, A. (2023). The role of Sami culture in creating sustainable cultural value for tourists - A case study of Jokkmokk's winter market. In L. Zsolnai, T. Walker, & P. Shrivastava (Eds.), *Value creation for a sustainable world: Innovating for ecological regeneration and human flourishing* (pp. 103–117). Palgrave-Macmillan.
Vetlesen, A. J. (2015). *The denial of nature. Environmental philosophy in the era of global capitalism*. Routledge.
Zsolnai, L. (1999). Limited wants, unlimited means: John Gowdy on primitive economies. *International Journal of Social Economics*, *26*(5–6), 832–833.
Zsolnai, L. (2015). *Post-materialistic business: Spiritual value-orientation in renewing management*. Palgrave.

Part II
Business in the Anthropocene

Chapter 7
Misfunctions and Blind Spots of Mainstream Businesses

Decades ago, David Korten (1995) observed that "corporations rule the world." This is more true today than ever before. Corporations are the most powerful players in the Anthropocene era and are mainly responsible for the biosphere's degraded state. Corporations and other mainstream business organizations produce financial wealth for their owners at the expense of nature, society, and future generations.

The key problem is the nature, form, and scale of mainstream business operations. The working models of today's mainstream businesses do not fit the reality of the biosphere. Mainstream business models vary, but none of them is compatible with the flourishing of life on Earth (including human, nonhuman, and future life). To achieve meaningful change in the humanity–nature nexus, we have to reinvent how businesses operate. The basic question is how business can become an ecologically conscious agent that operates within ecological and social limits, that is, uses only its "fair earth share" and contributes to the flourishing of human and nonhuman life on Earth (Shrivastava & Zsolnai, 2023).

Corporate misfunctioning forms a vicious circle in which the different elements intensify and aggravate one another, leading inexorably to a worsening of the situation (Fig. 7.1).

7.1 Shareholder Value/Profit Maximization

Financial wealth creation is considered the primary goal of corporations and other mainstream businesses. As Milton Friedman (1970) famously proclaimed, "the business of business is business." According to this position, the only responsibility of corporations is to increase their profits (and obey the law). To this day, many people, including professionals, believe that profit (or shareholder value) maximization is the legal duty of corporations, and that fulfilling this duty is the best way to serve the interests of business and society.

© The Author(s), under exclusive license to Springer Nature Switzerland AG 2026
L. Zsolnai, *Planet Positive Economy*, Springer Studies in Alternative Economics,
https://doi.org/10.1007/978-3-032-21131-6_7

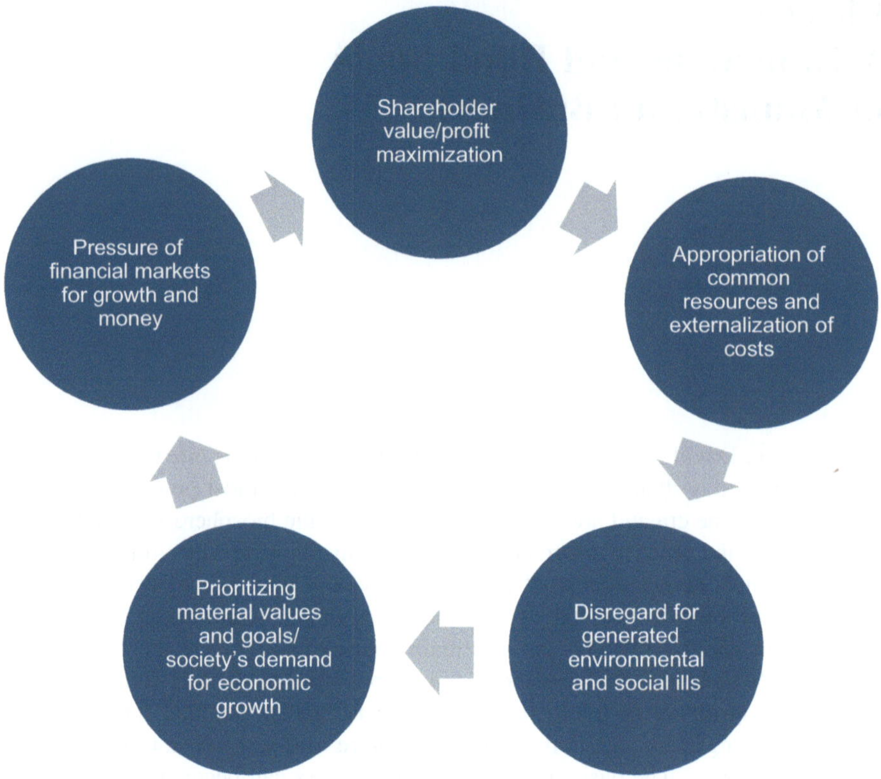

Fig. 7.1 The vicious circle of corporate misfunctioning. *Source* Author's creation

Awarding primacy to financial wealth creation is certainly the wrong approach. Widespread empirical evidence shows that following the shareholder value maximization model harms not only stakeholders and society at large but also shareholders themselves, both individually and immediately, and collectively and over time (Stout, 2012). Also, shareholder wealth is distinct from company health, and the latter should be the primary concern of those who manage corporations. This shift from a shareholder-centered to a company-centered perspective could make companies less vulnerable to damaging forms of activist investing and easier for managers to focus on the long term (Bower & Paine, 2017).

Due to their extreme focus on and "addiction" to financial wealth creation, corporations commit the so-called "error of the third kind," which means "solving the wrong problem precisely" (Mitroff & Silvers, 2009). Substantive failures occur when corporations and other mainstream businesses define their raison d'être as financial wealth creation, develop solutions to the wrong problems, and then fool themselves and others into believing they have solved the right problem to begin with.

7.2 Appropriating Common Resources and Externalizing Costs

Corporations create considerable value for society by satisfying customers' wants, creating jobs, and driving technological innovation. However, the currently dominant business models—i.e., the way businesses create value—are largely destructive. In many cases, corporations are "free riders" on society and nature, appropriating value from common natural and societal resources without paying the price, and externalizing most of the costs of their operations onto society, nature, and future generations (Sethi, 2013; Marquis, 2024).

The market economy as a whole is disembedded from society and nature (Polanyi, 1944). In parallel, mainstream business organizations, especially corporations, are also disembedded from the environmental and social context in which they operate and display no real interest in the places where they function. The core of the problem lies in the nature of the corporation itself (Bakan, 2003; Mayer, 2013; Stout, 2012).

The modern corporation as a legal entity was an institutional innovation in the early capitalist era. While it has considerable merits, such as serving as a means to collect and unite into one organization the small investments of many individuals, it also has the awkward side effect of dispersing and, ultimately, mitigating responsibility and accountability. In the form of limited liability companies, corporations allow their owners to limit their obligations associated with business activities to the amount of capital they have subscribed. Limited liability also means limited moral liability. "The situation may be contrasted with the case of unincorporated businesses, where unlimited liability also means unlimited moral liability. No distinction can be made by the business and the person(s) conducting it because the reputation of the one is the same as the reputation of the other" (Róna, 2013: 10). By their institutional nature, corporations and their owners have only limited responsibility (O'Higgins & Zsolnai, 2017).

Corporations exacerbate the consequences of globalization, which stem from separating corporate decisions and stakeholders, owners and workers, and consumers and the places of production. This facilitates the externalization of costs (that is, the creation of social and environmental problems and damage). Profit maximization and competitive pressures are the guiding principles of decisions throughout the supply chain. Globalization, therefore, contributes to masking the impacts of business activities and the externalization of production costs (Princen, 1997).

7.3 Disregarding Environmental and Social Ills

Due to their functioning, corporations—mostly unintentionally and indirectly—create environmental and social "ills." Corporations often develop blind spots to avoid recognizing the environmental and social harm caused by their activities.

Corporations produce “dirty things” and, at the same time, disengage from the unethical consequences of their conduct (Bandura et al., 2000). This is achieved through selective disengagement from moral self-sanctioning for transgressive conduct.

The mechanisms of moral disengagement enable otherwise considerate people and organizations to commit transgressive acts without experiencing personal distress. Moral disengagement mechanisms have been documented in famous business scandals (Bandura et al., 2000) and in the practices of major industries such as the gun, entertainment, tobacco, and financial industries (Bandura, 2015).

People and organizations do not ordinarily engage in reprehensible conduct until they have justified to themselves the rightness of their actions. In this process of moral justification, detrimental conduct is made personally and socially acceptable by portraying it as in the service of valued social or moral purposes (Bandura et al., 2000).

Euphemistic labeling provides a convenient tool for masking reprehensible activities or even conferring a respectable status upon them. Through sanitized and convoluted verbiage, destructive conduct is made benign, and those who engage in it are relieved of a sense of agency (Bandura et al., 2000).

By exploiting advantageous comparison, injurious conduct can be rendered benign or made to appear to have little consequence. The more flagrant the contrasted activities, the more likely it is that one’s own injurious conduct will appear trifling or even benevolent (Bandura et al., 2000).

Under conditions of the displacement of responsibility, people and organizations view their actions as springing from the social pressures or dictates of others rather than as something for which they are personally responsible. Because they are not the actual agents of their actions, they are spared self-censuring reactions. Hence, they are willing to behave in ways they would normally repudiate (e.g., if a legitimate authority accepted responsibility for the effects of its activities) (Bandura et al., 2000).

The exercise of moral control is also weakened when agency is obscured by the diffusion of responsibility for detrimental conduct. Any harm done by a group can always be attributed largely to the behavior of others. People behave more cruelly when they are held accountable as a group than when they are personally accountable for their actions (Bandura et al., 2000).

Additional ways of weakening self-deterring reactions operate by disregarding or distorting the consequences of action. When people and organizations pursue activities harmful to others for gain or for social recognition, they avoid facing the harm they cause or minimize it. In addition to selective inattention and the cognitive distortion of effects, such misrepresentation may involve active efforts to discredit evidence of any harm that is caused (Bandura et al., 2000).

Self-censure associated with injurious conduct can be disengaged or blunted by dehumanization that divests people of human qualities or attributes bestial qualities to them. Once dehumanized, they are no longer viewed as persons with feelings, hopes, and concerns but as subhuman objects (Bandura et al., 2000).

Blaming one’s adversaries or compelling circumstances is still another expedient that can serve self-exonerating purposes. In moral disengagement due to attribution of blame, people and organizations view themselves as faultless victims driven to injurious conduct by forcible provocation. By fixing the blame on others or on circumstances, not only are one's own injurious actions excusable, but one can even feel self-righteous in the process (Bandura et al., 2000).

7.4 Society's Demand for Economic Growth

Despite the well-known environmental, social, and psychological flaws of economic growth, society demands more GDP growth in response to perceived environmental and social ills. This is due to the strong materialist value orientation that characterizes Western and Westernizing societies today.

A materialist value orientation prioritizes values and goals such as money, power, sensual pleasure, and recognition (Kasser, 2003). These values and goals have no "natural limits," and pursuing them can become "toxic" as they are highly addictive (Brooks, 2022). Extensive psychological research shows that the more people prioritize materialistic goals, the lower their personal wellbeing and the more likely they are to engage in manipulative, competitive, and ecologically degrading behaviors. These findings regarding the negative association between materialistic values and personal wellbeing have been replicated across many settings with diverse samples from North America, Europe, and Asia (Kasser, 2011).

The strong materialist value orientation of today's societies creates the phenomenon of the "iron cage of consumerism," which fuels the demand for economic growth. Tim Jackson (2022) observes that people's relentless search for social status locks them into an escalating spiral of consumerism. They believe that their place in the social world depends on their ability to participate in consumption. Jackson argues that the "restless desire of the consumer is the perfect complement for the restless innovation of the entrepreneur. Taken together, these two self-reinforcing processes are exactly what is needed to drive economic growth forward ... The 'iron cage of consumerism' is a system in which no one is free" (Jackson, 2022: 2).

Consumerism is a self-defeating strategy for individuals and societies alike. The basic problem with consumerism is that the satisfaction of the current preferences of consumers is not a guarantee that those preferences are "rational" (in the sense that their satisfaction leads to a good life over time, not to mention the wider environmental and social problems of such behaviors) (Skidelsky & Skidelsky, 2012; Skidelsky, 2024).

7.5 Pressure of Financial Markets

Financial markets put immense pressure on mainstream businesses to grow and make money. Nowadays, institutional investors, investment funds, and pension funds own the large majority of corporate shares. Those funds—generally corporations as well—are themselves managed to increase profits at any cost. Moreover, there are multiple intermediaries between individuals and the companies they own, including portfolios managed by fund managers, and brokers and advisors. These involve numerous conflicts of interest, which complicate financial services and distance investors from the companies they invest in. The financial crisis of 2008 revealed how derivatives and other complex financial products can indeed hide reality from the eyes of even experts. Nowadays, investors choose between investment portfolios offered by their banks or agents, and are rarely knowledgeable about how their money works or what it does (Kay, 2015).

The financial system also acts as a principal evaluator of corporate performance. Shareholder value is constructed by the financial market and its institutions—rating agencies, consulting firms, auditors, and, finally, the stock market itself—a complex institutional infrastructure that purports to evaluate corporate performance and forces companies into an arms race for profit. Without a constant effort to increase profits and reduce costs, companies are threatened with losses in shareholder value and will finally be discredited. One of the most effective ways to reduce costs is to externalize them by making nature, society, and future generations pay them.

References

Bakan, J. (2003). *The corporation. The pathological pursuit of profit and power*. Penguin.

Bandura, A. (2015). *Moral disengagement: How good people can do harm and feel good about themselves*. Palgrave-Macmillan.

Bandura, A., Caprara, G.-V., & Zsolnai, L. (2000). Corporate transgressions through moral disengagement. *Journal of Human Values*, *6*(1), 57–64.

Bower, J. L., & Paine, L. S. (2017). The error at the heart of corporate leadership. *Harvard Business Review*, 50–60.

Brooks, A. C. (2022). How to want less. The secret to satisfaction has nothing to do with achievement, money, or stuff. *The Atlantic 2022 March*.

Friedman, M. (1970). The social responsibility of business is to increase its profits. *The New York Times Magazine 1970. March 13*.

Jackson, T. (2022). Paradise lost? — the iron cage of consumerism. *The Jus Semper Global Alliance 2022. December*.

Kasser, T. (2003). *The high price of materialism*. MIT Press.

Kasser, T. (2011). Materialistic value-orientation. In L. Bouckaert & L. Zsolnai (Eds.), *The Palgrave handbook of spirituality and business* (pp. 204–211). Palgrave-Macmillan.

Kay, J. (2015). *Other people's money: Masters of the universe or servants of the people?* Profile Books.

Korten, D. (1995). *When corporations rule the world*. Kumarian Press.

Marquis, C. (2024). *The profiteers: How business privatizes profits and socializes costs*. PublicAffairs.

Mayer, C. (2013). *Firm commitment: Why the corporation is failing us?* Oxford University Press.

Mitroff, I., & Silvers, A. (2009). *Dirty rotten strategies - How we trick ourselves and others into solving the wrong problems precisely*. Stanford University Press.

O'Higgins, E., & Zsolnai, L. (2017). What is progressive business? In: E. O'Higgins & L. Zsolnai (Eds.), *Progressive business models: Creating sustainable and pro-social enterprise* (pp. 3–25). Palgrave-Macmillan.

Princen, T. (1997). The shading and distancing of commerce: When internalization is not enough. *Ecological Economics*, *20*(3), 235–253.

Polanyi, K. (1944). *The great transformation*. Beacon Press.

Róna, P. (2013, June 8). Ethics and the limited liability corporation. *Paper presented at the Economic and Financial Crisis and the Human Person Workshop at the Von Hügel institute*, University of Cambridge.

Sethi, P. (Ed.). (2013). *Globalization and self-regulation. The crucial role that corporate codes of conduct play in global business*. Palgrave-Macmillan.

Shrivastava, P., & Zsolnai, L. (2023). Value creation in the Anthropocene. In L. Zsolnai, T. Walker, & P. Shrivastava (Eds.), *Value creation for a sustainable world: Innovating for ecological regeneration and human flourishing* (pp. 3–18). Palgrave-Macmillan.

Skidelsky, R., & Skidelsky, E. (2012). *How much is enough? Money and the good life*. Other Press.

Skidelsky, E. (2024). Economics and the three faces of prudence. In P. Róna, L. Zsolnai, & A. Wincewicz-Price (Eds.), *Homo curator: Towards the ethics of consumption* (pp. 131–142). Springer.

Stout, L. (2012). *The shareholder value myth. How putting shareholders first harms investors, corporations, and the public*. Berrett-Koehler Publishing, Inc.

References

Chapter 8
The Virtuous Circle of Corporate Functioning

Regarding the recent wave of capitalism, Stuart Hart, a pioneer of corporate sustainability, critically states that the dominant corporate greening movement of recent decades has failed (Hart, 2024). Despite considerable efforts to align business strategy with adressing environmental and societal challenges, the state of the world has not improved; rather, it has deteriorated. Hart suggests that to achieve a sustainable future, corporations should go beyond shareholder primacy and remake capitalism by focusing on societal and environmental purpose (Marquis, 2024).

This chapter reviews different directions of corporate reform, including the purpose model, B corporations, the Net Positive initiative, the conscious capitalism movement, the conception of sustainable capitalism, impact investing and the Long-Term Stock Exchange, and new measures of business performance. Then, an integrated vision for corporate "well-functioning" is presented, along with some leverage points for the required positive changes.

8.1 Directions of Corporate Reform

Regaining Purpose in Business

Oxford management scholar Colin Mayer argues that "It is the purposes of companies that determine both their structure and conduct which in turn determine their performance measured in relation to their purposes. It is only once one has defined a company's purposes that one can ascertain either its appropriate structure and conduct or its performance" (Mayer, 2018: 23).

The British Academy's (2018) research project "The Future of the Corporation" starts with the observation that over the last 50 years, corporate purpose has come to be equated solely with profit-making. This shift from public to private purpose

© The Author(s), under exclusive license to Springer Nature Switzerland AG 2026
L. Zsolnai, *Planet Positive Economy*, Springer Studies in Alternative Economics,
https://doi.org/10.1007/978-3-032-21131-6_8

"has been damaging for corporations' role in society, trust in business and the impact that business has had on the environment, inequality and social cohesion" (British Academy, 2018: 8).

The British Academy (2018) suggests reconceptualizing the corporation around the idea of "purpose." They have developed three principles to guide businesses in this: (1) corporate purpose should relate to the firm's wider contribution to public interests and societal goals; (2) corporations should develop a commitment to trustworthiness by creating reciprocal benefits for the firm, its stakeholders, and society; and (3) corporations should develop an enabling culture that clearly articulates values adopted consistently in the work of the corporation (British Academy, 2018: 8).

B Corporations

A "B Corporation" (B Corp) is a for-profit corporation certified for its social and environmental performance by B Lab, a global certification organization. To be granted this certification and to maintain it, companies must integrate their commitments to their stakeholders into their governing documents. Companies must recertify every 3 years to retain B Corporation status.

In January 2025, there were 9487 certified B Corporations across 160 industries in 104 countries. Notable companies with B Corp status include Nespresso, Ben & Jerry's, The Body Shop, Danone, Natura & Co., Patagonia, Inc., Seventh Generation Inc., and Weleda (B Lab, 2025).

B Corporations function as a force for good. They seek to transform the global economy into a more inclusive, equitable, and regenerative system. The stakeholder governance of B Corporations ensures that the actions of the companies benefit all stakeholders—customers, employees, suppliers, communities, and investors. B Corporations also aim to address the fundamental injustice, inequity, and violence that disproportionately impact people of color and women (B Lab, 2025).

B Corporations can obtain the benefits that socially responsible businesses usually do. Behavioral economist Frank (2004) showed that socially responsible firms can survive in competitive environments because social responsibility generates substantial benefits.

Moral considerations are not externally forced upon B Corporations; rather, they are internally chosen by them. As caring organizations, they are rewarded for the higher costs of their socially responsible behavior by their ability to form strong commitments among owners, managers, and employees and to establish trust-based relationships with customers and subcontractors (Frank, 2004).

The Net Positive Company

"Net Positive" is an initiative of Paul Polman, former CEO of Unilever, and business consultant Andrew Winston. It promotes the view that courageous companies can thrive by putting back more into society, the environment, and the global economy than they take out (Polman & Winston, 2021a).

The "Net Positive Manifesto" (Polman & Winston, 2021b) argues that corporate leaders can no longer treat human and planetary issues as "someone else's problem." For their own good, they must play an active role in addressing the biggest challenges of our time. The economy cannot thrive if people and the planet are not thriving.

The Net Positive company functions by helping the world flourish. Drawing on examples from Unilever and other leading companies, Polman and Winston (2021a) outline four critical paths for businesses to prosper today and win in the future. First, companies should operate in the service of multiple stakeholders, thereby benefiting investors (rather than putting shareholder interests above all others). Second, companies should take full ownership of all their impacts. Third, they should embrace deep partnerships, even with their critics. Fourth, companies should tackle systemic challenges by rethinking their advocacy and relationships with governments.

Polman and Winston (2021b) note that no company has yet reached the ambitious goal of becoming Net Positive. But a number of courageous companies have already begun this journey and are unlocking greater value for their businesses while helping solve larger problems for the benefit of all.

The Net Positive initiative is complemented and extended by the "Planet Positive" vision of the Institute of Electrical and Electronics Engineers (IEEE, 2023). This vision urges business and other professions to develop products, processes, and systems that conjointly serve the flourishing of human and nonhuman beings on Earth (Zsolnai et al., 2023).

Conscious Capitalism

The idea of "Conscious Capitalism" was developed by Whole Foods co-founder John Mackey and business scholar Raj Sisodia (Mackey & Sisodia, 2013). These prophets of conscious capitalism believe that businesses should operate ethically by serving the interests of all stakeholders, not just corporate management and shareholders. The guiding principles behind conscious capitalism are (1) higher purpose, (2) stakeholder orientation, (3) conscious leadership, and (4) conscious culture. Companies that embrace Conscious Capitalism include Whole Foods, Trader Joe's, and Starbucks (Kenton, 2024).

The credo of Conscious Capitalism suggests that free-market capitalism should be enriched by the assimilation of all common interests into a company's business plan. It acknowledges the relevance of competition, entrepreneurship, freedom to trade, the rule of law, and voluntary exchange, but suggests adding elements such as trust, compassion, collaboration, and value creation to the formula. Also, conscious capitalists believe that profit is the result of integrating the interests of all major stakeholders into company operations (Kenton, 2024).

The Conscious Capitalism movement is supported by the "Conscious Business Education" platform, which promotes teaching business models and practices that are purpose-driven, ethical, human-centered, sustainable, inclusive, and beneficial to all stakeholders (Conscious Business Education, 2025). Participating institutions include the Munich Business School, Barcelona School of Management, EGADE Business

School—Monterrey, the International Humanistic Management Association—New York City, and the Business Ethics Center of the Corvinus University of Budapest.

Critics of Conscious Capitalism say that this movement cannot solve the problems inherent to today's global capitalism. For example, the oversized ecological footprint of our economies can hardly be reduced by the voluntary actions of conscious companies alone. Also, market pressure often forces ethically oriented, conscious business leaders to behave in opportunistic ways (Zsolnai et al., 2022).

Sustainable Capitalism

"Sustainable Capitalism" is another idea for reinventing capitalism and the role of business. Hart (2024) forcefully argues against "shareholder primacy capitalism," which has become dangerous to society, the climate, and the planet. He believes that capitalism can be reformed and that a radically sustainable, just capitalism is possible, and even likely, in our lifetime.

Hart suggests that moving beyond "shareholder primacy" requires corporate transformations to re-embed purpose, and reforms to major economic institutions. In his view, a key requirement is to eliminate the "externalities" of the current capitalist system. "Sustainable capitalism will explicitly incorporate the needs of society and the planet, include a financial system that allows leaders to prioritize the planet, reorganize business schools around sustainable management thinking, and enable corporations not just to stop ignoring the damage they cause, but actually begin to create positive impact" (Hart, 2024: 5).

Critics of Sustainable Capitalism are not so optimistic. The Capital Institute (2025) states that regeneration, cooperation, and wellbeing are crucial aspects of sustainability that do not align with what capitalism has evolved into. Current capitalist practices may be reformed, but this will not change the fundamental incompatibility between sustainability and capitalism under the current model.

Impact Investing and the Long-Term Stock Exchange

Impact investing seeks to generate financial returns while also creating a positive social or environmental impact. Investors who engage in impact investing consider a company's commitment to corporate social responsibility or the duty to positively serve society as a whole (Chen, 2024).

Socially responsible investing (SRI) and environmental, social, and governance (ESG) investing are two main approaches to impact investing. Another example of impact investing is microfinance (small loans), which provides small-business owners with startup or expansion capital. The best-known impact investment funds include the Bill & Melinda Gates Foundation, the Soros Economic Development Fund, and the Ford Foundation.

Most impact investors seek returns comparable to market rates, but returns from impact investing tend to be slightly lower than the market average (Hand et al., 2021). However, impact investors are rewarded with moral satisfaction as their investments contribute to positive environmental and/or social change.

The concept of the Long-Term Stock Exchange was developed by Ries (2021). He says that today "companies want to innovate consistently, minimize pressure to hit short-term targets, join with long-term investors, and run their businesses with the stewardship that stakeholders and society demand" (Ries, 2021:5).

The Long-Term Stock Exchange commenced operations in the USA in 2020 as the only national securities exchange designed specifically to promote a long-term focus among investors and companies alike. To be eligible for listing on the Long-Term Stock Exchange, a company must adhere to five key principles. These are (1) serving the interests of a broad group of stakeholders, (2) measuring success over long time horizons that stretch from years to decades, (3) implementing compensation plans for executives and directors that reward long-term performance, (4) giving directors a crucial role in the setting of strategy, and (5) monitoring progress and engaging with long-term shareholders (Kolakowski, 2022).

Listing with the Long-Term Stock Exchange shows a company's commitment to a long-term time horizon in a transparent way that investors can consider when valuing the company, and that employees, customers, and communities can take seriously. Leading financial backers of the Long-Term Stock Exchange include the Founders Fund, Collaborative Fund, Andreessen Horowitz, Obvious Ventures, Uprising, and Initialized (LTSE, 2025).

New Measures of Business Performance

The British Academy (2018) urges the development of new measures for assessing the performance of businesses in a broad, multidimensional context. They say that "Most current measures of corporate purpose are accounting measures of material and financial capital and profit. Public purposes also require holistic action-guiding measures for environmental, social, and governance impacts" (British Academy, 2018: 17).

There are many new initiatives in environmental and social accounting and auditing, but the most radical among them is Economy for the Common Good (2020). Founder of the movement, Felber (2015), suggests that it makes sense for companies and social organizations to create a so-called "Common Good Balance Sheet," which shows the extent to which an organization abides by values like human dignity, solidarity, environmental sustainability, and transparency.

The Common Good Matrix assesses and scores the contribution of a business or social organization to the common good (Fig. 8.1). The categories in the columns are values related to successful relationships and a good life. The rows list the most important stakeholder groups of an organization. At the intersections of values and stakeholder groups, 20 "common good themes" describe and evaluate the organization's contribution to the common good.

The Common Good Balance Sheet methodology is far from perfect, but it can provide a comprehensive and multifaceted view of how well an organization is performing for a wide range of stakeholders in social and ecological respects. Since the scores can be positive or negative in each category, the matrix captures the real complexity of organizational functioning.

COMMON GOOD MATRIX 5.0

VALUE / STAKEHOLDER	HUMAN DIGNITY	SOLIDARITY AND SOCIAL JUSTICE	ENVIRONMENTAL SUSTAINABILITY	TRANSPARENCY AND CO-DETERMINATION
A: SUPPLIERS	**A1** Human dignity in the supply chain	**A2** Solidarity and social justice in the supply chain	**A3** Environmental sustainability in the supply chain	**A4** Transparency and co-determination in the supply chain
B: OWNERS, EQUITY- AND FINANCIAL SERVICE PROVIDERS	**B1** Ethical position in relation to financial resources	**B2** Social position in relation to financial resources	**B3** Use of funds in relation to social and environmental impacts	**B4** Ownership and co-determination
C: EMPLOYEES, INCLUDING CO-WORKING EMPLOYERS	**C1** Human dignity in the workplace and working environment	**C2** Self-determined working arrangements	**C3** Environmentally-friendly behaviour of staff	**C4** Co-determination and transparency within the organisation
D: CUSTOMERS AND OTHER COMPANIES	**D1** Ethical customer relations	**D2** Cooperation and solidarity with other companies	**D3** Impact on the environment of the use and disposal of products and services	**D4** Customer participation and product transparency
E: SOCIAL ENVIRONMENT	**E1** Purpose of products and services and their effects on society	**E2** Contribution to the community	**E3** Reduction of environmental impact	**E4** Social co-determination and transparency

Fig. 8.1 The common good balance sheet. *Source* Economy for the common good (2025). Reproduced with the permission of the international federation for the economy for the common good (http://www.Econgood.Org)

8.2 The Virtuous Circle of Corporate Well-Functioning

Considering the above-reported directions of corporate reform, an integrated model for corporate well-functioning can be developed. In the model, the elements form a *virtuous circle* in which one desirable outcome leads to another, potentially resulting in a continuous process of improvement (Fig. 8.2).

Sustainable Value Creation

A well-functioning business has a purpose related to sustainable value creation, which means the company is managed for all stakeholders, not just one particular group (e.g., shareholders or owners). *Sustainable value creation* is the development of products, processes, organizations, and actions that satisfy real human needs and have a positive impact on nature, society, and future generations. This implies that the functioning of a company is serving human wellbeing while contributing to the ecological regeneration of nature (Shrivastava & Zsolnai, 2022, 2023). Patagonia, Inc. is an example of a company engaged in sustainable value creation and managing for all stakeholders. As discussed earlier, Patagonia promotes simple and frugal lifestyles and uses business to protect and restore natural ecosystems.

Table 8.1 shows the main characteristics of Patagonia, Inc.

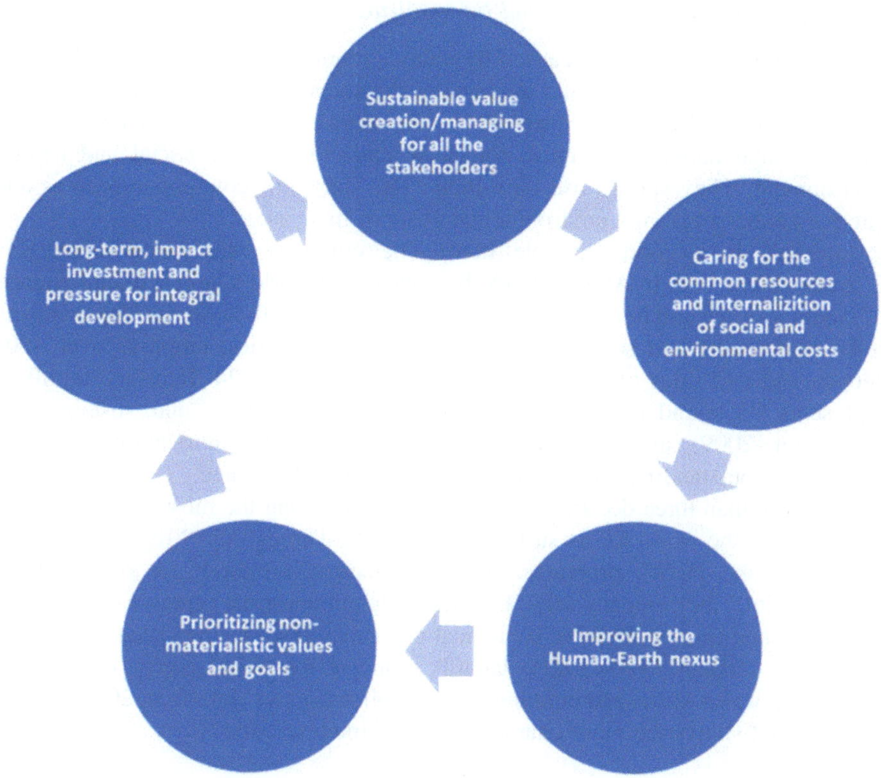

Fig. 8.2 The virtuous circle of corporate well-functioning. *Source* Author's creation

Table 8.1 Characteristics of Patagonia, Inc

	Values	Purpose	Strategy	Outcomes
Patagonia, Inc. (USA)	The ethos of nature-respecting mountaineering and Zen Buddhism	Producing the best outdoor clothing products and apparel without causing unnecessary harm to nature, and using business to protect and restore natural ecosystems	Minimalist style, transparency, innovation in retailing of ecological outdoor clothing and apparel, "activist company" that develops consumer consciousness and supports environmental movements	Monitoring and reducing the carbon footprint of the company; material, product, and value chain innovations; participation in regenerative agriculture, and buying large areas of wild nature in Patagonia, Chile

Source Author's creation

Caring for Common Resources and Internalizing Social and Environmental Costs

One of the biggest problems caused by today's mainstream businesses is that they overuse common resources and externalize the social and environmental costs of their functioning. Businesses must not be free riders on human, social, cultural, and environmental capital, and must not cause emissions to the social and natural environment. They should use only their "fair share" of common resources and internalize the social and environmental costs of their use.

Interface is a good example here. The company was founded by Ray C. Anderson in 1973 in Atlanta, USA. It is one of the world's largest manufacturers of modular office and household carpet, floor mats, and office fabric. The company sells its products and services in more than 100 countries, employs over 4000 people, and had sales of more than 1.3 billion USD in 2024. Interface faithfully represents its founder's commitment to industrial ecology and sustainability (Anderson, 2009), and is known for significant industry innovations, valuable brands, and outstanding social and environmental performance.

For more than three decades, Interface has been among the most well-recognized companies in the world for its sustainability efforts. Through its "Mission Zero" and "Climate Take Back" programs, and its attempts to climb its own "Mount Sustainability," the company seeks to completely eliminate the negative effects of its operations and reverse negative ecological processes. Interface has been particularly focused on sending zero waste to landfill, reducing fossil fuel energy use to zero, eliminating water waste, and emitting zero greenhouse gases (Interface, 2025).

Table 8.2 shows the main characteristics of Interface, Inc.

Table 8.2 Characteristics of interface, Inc

	Values	Purpose	Strategy	Outcomes
Interface, Inc. (USA)	Industrial ecology, purpose-driven and restorative economy, consciousness, compassion, genuineness in doing business	Doing right for a positive future and showing that sustainability is good for business. Transforming itself into an agent of restoration and being a catalyst for the redesign of the industry	Globally producing commercial and household modular flooring, using "The Natural Step" sustainability methodology and the concept of "Mount Sustainability." Radical product and process innovation, close cooperation with members of the value chain	Programs to become carbon negative by 2040, to eliminate all negative impacts, a cyclical, gentle business model involving radical redesign of processes and products mimicking nature, and improvement of life for all stakeholders

Source Author's creation

Improving the Human-Earth Nexus

Over the last 50–70 years, mainstream businesses have significantly contributed to the ever-worsening trends associated with the Human-Earth nexus. Well-functioning companies should reverse these trends by developing multiple win–win solutions that are simultaneously beneficial for people, nature, future generations, and the companies themselves.

Organic India is an example of how a company can improve the Human-Earth nexus. It is a private limited liability company with 350 employees in Lucknow, Uttar Pradesh, India. Inspired by the simple life teachings of Papaji (a wise teacher, guide, and mentor), Prashanti de Jaeger and Bharat Mitra started a small business in the 1990s to provide Ayurvedic herbal formulations to support people's health and wellbeing. In 2006, the company was renamed Organic India and continues to stand for its values such as service to all, total integrity, commitment to quality, and respect and devotion to Mother Nature (Zsolnai, 2015).

The main product of Organic India is organic Tulsi teas. In addition, they produce Ayurvedic and medicinal herbs, as well as other organic foods and spices. The company has melded Indian health wisdom and cutting-edge technology to create premium products that ensure the maximum retention of potency and nutritional value. The company promotes holistic, sustainable development for all beings through organic agriculture, service, sanctity, and integrity. It helps farmers to regenerate the soil and make a decent living. Over the years, Organic India has evolved into a global leader in promoting organic products and supporting sustainable farming, wildcrafting, and village/tribal agricultural communities in India and beyond (Organic India, 2025).

Table 8.3 shows the main characteristics of Organic India.

Prioritizing Non-Materialist Values and Goals

Companies should not uncritically accept and support people's materialistic value orientation, which prioritizes money, sensual pleasure, status, and image. Rather, well-functioning companies can make efforts to change the materialistic mindset of their customers and other stakeholders by prioritizing nonmaterialist values and goals.

Table 8.3 Characteristics of Organic India

	Values	Purpose	Strategy	Outcomes
Organic India (India)	Hindu spirituality	Make Indian herbs in the Ayurveda tradition accessible to people while respecting Mother Nature in doing business	Producing and supplying genuine, organic products for sustainability-aware, healthy living	Creating fair and sustainable livelihoods for thousands of local farmers and contributing to the restoration of soil in India

Source Author's creation

Unilever is an example of a company that is helping customers and other stakeholders to prioritize nonmaterialist values and goals. Unilever PLC is a British/Dutch global consumer goods company whose "Sustainable Living Plan" includes three main goals: improving health and wellbeing, reducing environmental impact, and enhancing livelihoods. The Unilever Foundation improves quality of life through the provision of hygiene, sanitation, access to clean drinking water, basic nutrition, and improving self-esteem. Unilever promotes this through its partnerships with Oxfam, PSI, Save the Children, UNICEF, and the World Food Program (Unilever, 2025).

Unilever creates value for customers by supplying them with responsibly sourced products. It earns enough profit to be sustainable and supply the products that consumers demand, and it works to achieve the goals it has set for itself in the Sustainable Living Plan: to grow as a company while protecting the environment (Murphy & Murphy, 2018).

CEO Paul Polman joined Unilever in 2009 and served in this role until 2019. He eliminated earnings guidance and quarterly reporting and stated that he did not want hedge funds as investors, thereby changing the way Unilever does business. During Polman's tenure, Unilever delivered returns vastly superior to rivals and more than double those of the FTSE index. Unilever is working to develop solutions to various problem areas, including providing safe drinking water, fighting viruses, improving packaging, promoting sustainable washing, storing renewable energy, and changing consumer behavior (Murphy & Murphy, 2018).

Table 8.4 shows the main characteristics of Unilever.

Long-Term Impact Investment and Pressure for Integral Development

Investors and financial institutions should go beyond a short-term perspective and an extreme focus on financial returns. Corporate well-functioning requires investors and financial institutions with a long-term perspective and an active interest in promoting integral development.

Triodos Bank is an example of a company that practices long-term impact investment and applies pressure for the integral development of society. Triodos Bank is a public limited liability company with 1700 employees in the Netherlands. It is recognized as a pioneer of sustainable and ethical banking. Triodos only lends to organizations and invests in projects that benefit people, communities, and nature (Hofstra & Klosterman, 2018).

Table 8.4 Characteristics of Unilever

	Values	Purpose	Strategy	Outcome
Unilever UK/ The Netherlands	Universal humanism	To serve the health and wellbeing of the customers in a sustainable way	Educating customers and suppliers on sustainability and drastically reducing the company's operational footprint	Contributing to the quality of life of more than two billion people while halving the environmental impact of the company

Source Author's creation

Table 8.5 Characteristics of Triodos Bank

	Values	Purpose	Strategy	Outcome
Triodos Bank (The Netherlands)	Anthroposophy and vision of a sustainable society	Banking for positive social, environmental, and cultural change	Screening investments by using financial, social, and environmental criteria simultaneously	Financing more than 40,000 sustainability and community development projects over 30 years

Source Author's creation

The name of the bank, "Triodos," refers to "three ways," meaning the bank's operations are based on three pillars: people, planet, and profit. Projects are evaluated simultaneously against financial, social, and environmental criteria. Triodos finances companies, institutions, and projects that add cultural value and benefit people and the environment with the support of depositors and investors who wish to encourage social responsibility and a sustainable society. It is influenced by the anthroposophical movement (Triodos Bank, 2025).

Table 8.5 shows the main characteristics of Triodos Bank.

Robert Frank (2004) challenges the prevailing view in our era that competitive pressure makes it naïve to expect people and organizations to restrain themselves for the common good. The examples of well-functioning companies presented here illustrate how businesses can work for the common good while staying financially healthy.

References

Anderson, R. C. (2009). *Business lessons from a radical industrialist*. St. Martin's Griffin.

B Lab. (2025). https://www.bcorporation.net/en-us/. Accessed January 25, 2025.

British Academy. (2018). *Reforming business for the twenty-first century. A framework for the future of the corporation*. The British Academy of Sciences.

Capital Institute. (2025). https://capitalinstitute.org/. Accessed January 26, 2025.

Chen, J. (2024). *Impact investing: Definition, types, and examples*. Investopedia. September 20, 2024. https://www.investopedia.com/terms/i/impact-investing.asp. Accessed January 25, 2025.

Conscious Business Education. (2025). https://consciousbusinesseducation.com/. Accessed January 25, 2025.

Economy for the Common Good. (2025). https://www.ecogood.org/. Accessed January 27, 2025.

Felber, C. (2015). *Change everything: Creating an economy for the common good*. Zed Books.

Frank, R. (2004). *What price the moral high ground? Ethical dilemmas in competitive environments*. Princeton University Press.

Hand, D., Sunderji, S., Nova, N. and De, I. (2021). *Impact investing decision-making: Insights on financial performance*. Global Impact Investing Network January 14, 2021. https://thegiin.org/publication/research/impact-investing-decision-making-insights-on-financial-performance/. Accessed January 26, 2025.

Hart, S. (2024). *Beyond shareholder primacy: Remaking capitalism for a sustainable future*. Stanford University Press.

Hofstra, N. & Kloosterman, L. (2018). Banking on values: Triodos Bank. In E. O'Higgins & L. Zsolnai (Eds.), *Progressive business models. Creating sustainable and pro-social enterprise* (pp. 29–50). Palgrave-Macmillan.

IEEE. (2023). *Strong Sustainability by Design. Prioritizing Ecosystem and Human Flourishing With Technology Based Solutions*. https://sagroups.ieee.org/planetpositive2030/our-work/. Accessed January 25, 2025.

Interface. (2025). https://www.interface.com/US/en-US.html. Accessed January 28, 2025.

Kenton, W. (2024). Conscious capitalism: Definition, 4 principles, and company examples *Investopedia*. https://www.investopedia.com/terms/c/conscious-capitalism.asp. Accessed January 25, 2025.

Kolakowski, M. (2022). *Long-term stock exchange (LTSE): What it is, how it works*. Investopedia. https://www.investopedia.com/long-term-stock-exchange-ltse-5077275. Accessed January 26, 2025.

LTSE. (2025). https://ltse.com/. Accessed January 26, 2025.

Mackey, J. & Sisodia, R. (2013). *Conscious capitalism: Liberating the heroic spirit of business*. Harvard Business Review Press.

Marquis, C. (2024). *Stuart hart on how to move beyond shareholder primacy*. Forbes June 9, 2024. https://www.forbes.com/sites/christophermarquis/2024/06/09/stuart-hart-on-how-to-move-beyond-shareholder-primacy/. Accessed January 17, 2025.

Mayer, C. (2018). *Prosperity. Better business makes the greater good*. Oxford University Press.

Murphy, P. E. & Murphy, C. E. (2018). Sustainable living: Unilever. In Eleanor O'Higgins & Laszlo Zsolnai (Eds.), *Progressive business models. Creating sustainable and pro-social enterprise* (pp. 263–286). Palgrave-Macmillan.

Organic India. (2025). https://www.organicindia.com/. Accessed January 28, 2025.

Polman, P. & Winston, A. (2021a). *Net positive: How courageous companies thrive by giving more than they take*. Harvard Business Review Press.

Polman, P. & Winston, A. (2021b). The net positive manifesto. *Harvard Business Review* 2021 September-October. https://hbr.org/2021/09/the-net-positive-manifesto. Accessed January 25, 2025.

Ries, E. (2021). *The lean startup: How today's entrepreneurs use continuous innovation to create radically successful businesses*. Crown Business.

Shrivastava, P. & Zsolnai, L. (2022). Wellbeing oriented organizations: Connecting human flourishing with ecological regeneration. *Business Ethics, the Environment & Responsibility*, *31*(2), 386–397.

Shrivastava, P. & Zsolnai, L. (2023). Value creation in the Anthropocene. In L. Zsolnai, T. Walker, & P. Shrivastava (Eds.), *Value creation for a sustainable world: Innovating for ecological regeneration and human flourishing* (pp. 3–18). Palgrave-Macmillan.

Triodos Bank. (2025). https://www.triodos.com/. Accessed January 28, 2025.

Unilever. (2025). https://www.unilever.com/. Accessed January 28, 2025.

Zsolnai, L. (2015). *Post-materialistic business: Spiritual value-orientation in renewing management*. Palgrave.

Zsolnai, L., Flanagan, B. & Bouckaert, L. (2022). Spirituality and ethics: Editorial for the special section. *Journal of Management, Spirituality & Religion*, *19*(3), 234–236.

Zsolnai, L., Walker, T. & Shrivastava, P. (Eds.). (2023). *Value creation for a sustainable world: Innovating for ecological regeneration and human flourishing*. Palgrave-Macmillan.

Part III
Models for Wellbeing Creation

Chapter 9
Living with Non-Materialistic Values

This chapter discusses the negative consequences of the materialistic value orientation that dominates today's economic and business practices. It is argued that for achieving a planet-positive economy, a spiritual value orientation should be adopted that gives priority to nonmaterial values over material ones. Finally, the so-called "Pascal's Wager" is revisited to show the reasonableness of opting for spirituality rather than materialism.

9.1 The High Price of Materialism

In his influential book *The High Price of Materialism*, American psychologist Tim Kasser (2002) analyzes how our contemporary culture of consumerism and materialism affects the happiness and psychological health of people. Kasser investigates how people's materialistic desires relate to their well-being. He shows that people whose values center on the accumulation of wealth or material possessions face a greater risk of unhappiness, including anxiety, depression, low self-esteem, and problems with intimacy—regardless of age, income, or culture. Drawing on a decade's worth of empirical data, Kasser shows that materialistic values actually undermine people's well-being, as they perpetuate feelings of insecurity, weaken the ties that bind them, and make them feel less free.

As we have already emphasized, a materialistic value orientation gives priority to goals such as money, possessions, image, and status (Kasser, 2011). This involves "attaining financial success, having nice possessions, having the right image (produced, in large part, through consumer goods), and having a high status (defined mostly by the size of one's pocketbook and the scope of one's possessions)" (Kasser et al., 2004: 13). Research shows that the more people focus on materialistic goals, the less they tend to care about spiritual goals. Furthermore, numerous studies document that the more people prioritize materialistic goals, not

© The Author(s), under exclusive license to Springer Nature Switzerland AG 2026

L. Zsolnai, *Planet Positive Economy*, Springer Studies in Alternative Economics,
https://doi.org/10.1007/978-3-032-21131-6_9

only the lower their personal wellbeing, but the more likely they are to engage in manipulative, competitive, and ecologically degrading behaviors (Kasser, 2011).

A major problem with pursuing material goals is the *addictive nature* of those goals. Brooks (2022) recalls that theologian and philosopher Saint Thomas Aquinas rightly states that attachment to money, power, pleasure, and honor cannot give satisfaction, and the agent wishes to have more of them. Hence, an addictive spiral is created (Brooks, 2022). Saint Thomas Aquinas also notes that the craving for money, power, pleasure, and honor has no natural limits, so addiction to them is unbounded.

Also, a materialistic value orientation often leads to what is called "toxic behavior." *Toxic behavior* is characterized by actions and attitudes that harm or manipulate others. This is not a surprise because empirical research shows that "to the extent people take on materialistic values and beliefs, they are less likely to behave in ways that promote the well-being of other people, and they may actually behave in ways that hurt others" (Kasser, 2011: 207–208).

The behavior of some of today's businessmen and politicians clearly illustrates the dangerous, addictive, and toxic nature of a strong materialistic value orientation.

9.2 The Benefits of a Spiritual Value Orientation

The great spiritual traditions of humanity unanimously reject the materialistic value orientation. For example, the *Bible* teaches, "Do not store up for yourselves treasure on earth, where it grows rusty and moth-eaten, and thieves break in to steal it. Store up treasure in heaven ... For wherever your treasure is, there will your heart be also" (Matthew 6:19–21). The *Bhagavad-Gita* (2.62–63) warns that "Pondering on objects of the senses gives rise to attraction; from attraction grows desire, desire flames to passion, passion breeds recklessness; and then betrayed memory lets noble purpose go and saps the mind, till purpose, mind, and man are all undone." Taoism likewise says, "Chase after money and security, and your heart will never unclench," and "He who knows he has enough is rich" (Kasser, 2011: 209–210).

A spiritual value orientation deemphasizes the value of pursuing material goods and prioritizes nonmaterial goals such as love, compassion, caring for others, and transcendence. A spiritual value orientation may emerge as a result of spontaneous spiritual experiences or spiritual exercises.

Transpersonal psychology has documented that spiritual experiences involve authentic experimental identification with other people, animals, plants, and various other aspects of nature and the cosmos. "We typically undergo profound changes in our understanding of existence and of the nature of reality. We directly experience the divine, sacred, or numinous dimensions of existence in a compelling way" (Grof, 1998: 2).

Despite the rich diversity of spiritual experience, the main ethical message is always the same: love and compassion, deep reverence for life, and empathy with all sentient beings. Spiritual experiences allow people to "develop a new system of values that is not based on conventional norms, precepts, commandments, and fear of punishment" but on an "understanding of the universal order" (Grof, 1998: 129). People realize that they are an integral part of creation and that by hurting others, they hurt themselves.

A spiritual value orientation produces beneficial effects for the people and the planet. Spirituality is good for the health and well-being of people and fosters pro-social and ecologically friendly behavior.

Lisa Miller (2021) at Columbia University Medical School has studied the brain structures of depressed and nondepressed people to see how spirituality is associated with brain structure and correlated with the risk of depression. Their magnetic resonance imaging (MRI) findings show that "the high-spiritual brain was healthier and more robust than the low-spiritual brain. And the high-spiritual brain was thicker and stronger in exactly the same regions that weaken and wither in depressed brains" (Miller, 2021: 13). Accordingly, it appears that spirituality protects people against mental suffering.

Psychological studies have found that higher levels of spirituality are associated with higher levels of well-being (positive affect, purpose in life, positive relations with others, personal growth, self-acceptance, environmental mastery, and autonomy) (Greenfield et al., 2009). Other studies have found that spirituality (in the form of spiritual and physical oneness) is positively associated with proenvironmental attitudes (Greenfield et al., 2009). Spirituality also predicts the propensity to donate to a pro-environmental group (Garfield et al., 2014).

The scientific results reported here support the position that we need to develop and promote business and economic working models that are based on or at least compatible with spiritual value orientation. These kinds of working models can catalyze progress towards a planet-positive economy.

9.3 "Pascal's Wager" Revisited

The spiritual value orientation is incompatible with the materialistic value orientation. Psychological research suggests that materialistic and spiritual values are in direct opposition (Burroughs & Rindfleisch, 2002). A large-scale cross-cultural study of 1800 subjects from 15 cultures (Grouzet et al., 2005) shows that the goal of spirituality is most strongly opposed by the goal of hedonism, or the concern with sensual pleasure. The goal of financial success was also found to be in psychological opposition to spiritual goals (Kasser, 2011: 210).

The spiritual traditions of humanity also suggest that it is impossible to simultaneously pursue spiritual and materialistic goals. Jesus puts this so succinctly: "No one can serve two masters. Either you will hate the one and love the other, or you

Table 9.1 Pascal's Wager

	God exists	God does not exist
Believing in God	Infinite gain	Finite loss
Disbelieving in God	Infinite loss	Finite gain

Source Author's creation

Table 9.2 Materialistic versus spiritual value orientation

	Expected material reward	Expected spiritual reward
Materialistic value orientation	Mm	Ms
Spiritual value orientation	Sm	Ss

Source Author's creation

will be devoted to the one and despise the other. You cannot serve both God and money" (Matthew 6:24).

Spirituality is an option, and materialism is also an option. However, we have reason to make a choice between them.

French mathematician and philosopher Blaise Pascal (1623–1662) developed an argument about the existence of God in the form of a bet. This is the so-called "Pascal's Wager." Table 9.1 shows the payoffs of the bet.

According to decision theory, the only value that matters in the matrix is "infinite gain." The other values of the matrix are either negative or finite. So the only rational decision is to choose the option of "Believing in God." Hence, Pascal's Wager suggests that it is better to live as though God exists (Hájek, 2012).

Inspired by Pascal's Wager, a payoff matrix can be developed to show the material and spiritual rewards of choosing between a materialistic value orientation and a spiritual value orientation. (Table 9.2).

Mm is usually greater than **Sm,** and **Ms** is usually smaller than **Ss,** but scientific evidence suggests that [**Sm, Ss**] brings greater satisfaction for people than [**Mm, Ms**]. People who follow a spiritual value orientation are usually happier and healthier and live lives that are more beneficial to society and nature than people who follow a materialistic value orientation.

So choosing spirituality over materialism in the conduct of one's life is reasonable.

References

Burroughs, J. E., & Rindfleisch, A. (2002). Materialism and well-being: A conflicting values perspective. *Journal of Consumer Research*, *29*(3), 348–370.

Brooks, A. C. (2022). How to want less. *The Atlantic*, March 2022.

Garfield, A. M., Drwecki, B. B., Moore, C. F., Kortenkamp, K. V. & Gracz, M. D. (2014). The oneness beliefs scale: Connecting spirituality with pro-environmental behavior. *Journal for the Scientific Study of Religion*, *53*(2), 356–372.

Greenfield, E. A., Vaillant, G. E., & Marks, N. F. (2009). Do formal religious participation and spiritual perceptions have independent linkages with diverse dimensions of psychological well-being?. *Journal of Health and Social Behavior*, *50*(2), 196–212.

Grof, S. (1998). *The cosmic game. Explorations of the frontiers of human consciousness*. State University of New York Press.

Grouzet, F. M. E., Kasser, T., Ahuvia, A., Fernandez-Dols, J. M., Kim, Y., Lau, S., Ryan, R. M., Saunders, S., Schmuck, P. & Sheldon, K. M. (2005). The structure of goal contents across fifteen cultures. *Journal of Personality and Social Psychology*, *89*(5), 800–816.

Hájek, A. (2012). Pascal's wager. *Stanford Encyclopedia of Philosophy*. https://plato.stanford.edu/entries/pascal-wager/. Accessed October 1, 2025.

Kasser, T. (2002). *The high price of materialism*. MIT Press.

Kasser, T. (2011). Materialistic value-orientation. In L. Bouckaert & L. Zsolnai (Eds.), *The Palgrave handbook of spirituality and business* (pp. 204–211). Palgrave-Macmillan.

Kasser, T., Ryan, R. M., Couchman, C. E., & Sheldon, K. M. (2004). Materialistic values: Their causes and consequences. In T. Kasser & A. D. Kanner (Eds.), *Psychology and consumer culture: The struggle for a good life in a materialistic world* (pp. 11–28). American Psychological Association.

Miller, L. (2021). *The awakened brain. The psychology of spirituality and our search for meaning*. Random House.

Chapter 10
Self-Interest or Higher Purpose?

The central proposition of this chapter is that the self-interest doctrine of modern economics should be changed. To serve public happiness and ecological sustainability, it is necessary to prioritize intrinsic (ethical) motivation over extrinsic (financial) motivation. The Civil Economy tradition can help us to do this.

The chapter uses the case of modern agribusiness as an *experimentum crucis* to show the devastating effects of the self-interest-based functioning of modern mainstream corporations. As an alternative, the case of Slow Food is presented. A preliminary conclusion is that we may expect healthy, ecological food to be created not out of the self-interest of business actors, but from a passion for creating beautiful food and preserving the land and its cultural traditions.

The chapter also discusses the so-called "crowding effect" in the economic context. Under specific conditions, market coordination may "crowd out" ethical motivation by shifting the frame of reference from moral considerations to cost-benefit calculations. Fortunately, there are also conditions under which ethical motivation may "crowd in" market coordination—when cost-benefit calculations strengthen moral considerations.

The chapter explores the civil economy model, where the ultimate goal is not profit-making but achieving public happiness, the basic strategy is not exploitation but sharing, the main organizing principle is not market exchange but mutual reciprocity, the governing form is not hierarchy but participation, the type of rationality is not efficiency but relationality, and the criterion of success is not individual wealth creation but creating value for all stakeholders.

The conclusion of the chapter is that we need to develop economic arrangements that combine ethics and the market in a mutually supportive way. Acting in line with a higher purpose should precede acting from self-interest in business and economic life if the flourishing of humans and nonhuman others matters.

© The Author(s), under exclusive license to Springer Nature Switzerland AG 2026
L. Zsolnai, *Planet Positive Economy*, Springer Studies in Alternative Economics,
https://doi.org/10.1007/978-3-032-21131-6_10

10.1 Introduction

This chapter is dedicated to the personality and scientific achievements of Professor Stefano Zamagni. He is Professor of Economics at the University of Bologna and former President of the Pontifical Academy of Social Sciences. I have been collaborating with him for more than 30 years, so some personal remarks may be appropriate here.

My collaboration with Stefano Zamagni began in 1993 when we published the Hungarian version of the book *Social and Ethical Aspects of Economics* (Musu & Zamagni, 1990). This Hungarian translation (Musu & Zamagni, 1993) was prepared for the opening of our Business Ethics Center in Budapest. Since then, Professor Zamagni has served on the International Advisory Board of our Center (BEC, 2025).

Over the years, I have collaborated with Professor Zamagni through a number of international conferences, workshops, and academic visits in Rome, Bologna, Sienna, Oxford, Leuven, Budapest, and elsewhere. I have helped publish his books and papers in various scientific outlets that I edited (Bruni & Zamagni, 2007, Zamagni, 2002, 2005, 2006, 2010, 2011a, 2011b, 2017). Also, it was my great honor that he authored a fine paper (Zamagni, 2018) for the *Liber Amicorum* (Bouckaert et al., 2018) book celebrating my 60th anniversary.

Stanford University organizational scientist James March once proclaimed that undermining the self-interest doctrine may be the most important project of the twenty-first century (March, 2011). This chapter investigates the relevance and applicability of the self-interest doctrine in the context of the current reality of the Anthropocene era, characterized by climate change, biodiversity loss, ecosystem collapse, welfare deficits, migration, and international conflict.

The central proposition of the chapter is that "greed is not good"—as the self-interested behavior of economic players destroys nature, reduces the well-being of people, and endangers the chance that future generations will live a decent life.

10.2 Who Will Produce Good Food for Us?

In his book, *The Wealth of Nations*, Smith (1776) famously stated that "It is not from the benevolence of the butcher, the brewer, or the baker, that we expect our dinner, but from their regard to their own interest" (Book I, Chapter II, para 2). I do not want to discuss the original meaning of this statement in the eighteenth-century context; rather, I am interested in investigating the relevance and applicability of the self-interest doctrine in today's world, where it is not individual butchers, brewers, and bakers who produce our food but giant multinational companies like Nestlé, Coca-Cola, and Kraft Heinz.

The method called "experimentum crucis" will be used to decide the merits of the self-interest doctrine in today's ecological, social, and economic circumstances. In science, the experimentum crucis (crucial experiment or critical experiment) is a method for deciding whether a particular hypothesis or theory is true. The experiment is designed so that it produces results that rule out a hypothesis or theory if it is false. The case of modern agribusiness (Zsolnai & Podmaniczky, 2010) will be taken to investigate the rightness of the self-interest doctrine.

The expression "modern agribusiness" refers to large-scale, industrialized, vertically integrated food production systems. It encompasses the entire chain of agriculture-related businesses, including the supply sector (seeds, agrichemicals, and machinery), the basic production sector (crop and animal husbandry), and the food industry/trade sector (food processing, storage, transport, distribution, marketing, advertising, and retail sales). The ultimate goal of corporate farming is to vertically integrate the entire food production process, from the development of proprietary strains of DNA to the distribution and sale of food to consumers. (Zsolnai & Podmaniczky, 2010).

Modern agribusiness poses dangers to both natural ecosystems and social communities, as well as to health. Contaminated with chemicals, the products of industrial agriculture are typically of low quality and have poor nutritional value. Improved technologies and greater industrial inputs do not necessarily lead to suitable solutions. The root of the problem is that modern agribusiness is—in the words of German classical economist Albert Thaer—"a form of industry, where the goal is to make profit by using products of plant and animal origin" (Zsolnai & Podmaniczky, 2010).

Striving for profit maximization, agricultural management systems have been created that, due to their negative environmental impact and other adverse effects, have made agriculture antagonistic to society's well-being and long-term interests. Industrial agricultural systems focus exclusively on production and neglect the biological and social functions of the landscape. Its methods and technologies are selected solely on the basis of efficiency, productivity, and profitability (Zsolnai & Podmaniczky, 2010).

Modern agribusiness generates significant economies of scale. It is criticized for its tendency to concentrate food production through methods designed to maximize crop yields. At the same time, through a process of vertical integration, corporate farming results in the concentration not only of the ownership of the means of production but also of the distribution and sale of the food that is produced (Zsolnai & Podmaniczky, 2010).

A critical consideration is whether the quality of the food that reaches the consumer is as good as it would be under alternative structures of ownership and production. To the extent that corporate farming primarily seeks to maximize profits, this may adversely affect nutritional value, freshness, and flavor, as well as the range of products available to consumers. Corporate farming practices may also involve the more widespread use of genetically modified crops, hormones, preservatives, color additives, and insecticides.

Modern agribusiness is disembedded from its environmental and social context and treats the natural environment and human persons as mere means to its own ends. The self-interest orientation of modern agribusiness produces profits and increases productivity at the expense of the environment, society, and human health.

An alternative conception of food production is "Slow Food," which suggests that the food we consume should be ecological, healthy, and beautiful. For this, the ecological quality of the land and the culture and traditions of local communities should be restored and preserved (Shrivastava & Zsolnai, 2022).

Slow Food is a movement with more than 100,000 members in Italy and abroad. The underlying vision of Slow Food is "eco-gastronomy." This innovative approach calls for an awareness of the cultural, historical, social, and ecological conditions and mechanisms that underpin the production of locally grown, high-quality food (Petrini & Padovani, 2005).

Eco-gastronomy recognizes the strategic linkages among people, planet, and plate. Local and sustainable food feeds people and respects the carrying capacity of the Earth while ensuring decent living conditions for farmers and quality enjoyment for consumers. Slow Food promotes food and wine culture by safeguarding and renewing the cultural heritage of local communities and the biodiversity of their land (Tencati & Zsolnai, 2012).

Slow Food requires innovative methods of production and consumption, which are: (i) small-scale, (ii) local, and (iii) slow (Tencati & Zsolnai, 2012). To pursue its goals, Slow Food has developed projects to disseminate best practices. These include the University of Gastronomic Sciences (UNISG), Salone Internazionale del Gusto (an international festival of flavor known as "The Ark of Taste"), and the Slow Food Foundation for Biodiversity.

The experiences of modern agribusiness and Slow Food suggest that Adam Smith's original statement should be corrected. In today's context, we can expect healthy, ecological food to come not from self-interested business players, but from those who have a passion for creating beautiful food and serving others.

10.3 Market and Ethics: The Crowding Effect

Based on his lifetime preoccupation with nonequilibrium economic systems, Kornai (1984, 1990, 1992) identified some of the basic coordination mechanisms that play a decisive role in the working of economic systems. These coordination mechanisms are market coordination, bureaucratic coordination, ethical coordination, and aggressive coordination.

Market coordination: There is a horizontal relationship between the buyer and the seller. They enter into the relationship voluntarily. Each of them is motivated to make a profit or surplus. The transaction is monetarized (Kornai, 1984).

Bureaucratic coordination: There is a hierarchical relationship (sub- and superordination) between the actors. Participation in the relationship is nonvoluntary.

Subordinate actors are motivated to accept the orders and prohibitions of superordinate actors through administrative coercion supported by legal sanctions. The relationship is lasting and institutionalized. (Kornai, 1984).

Ethical coordination: A horizontal relationship exists between the actors. They enter into the relationship on a voluntary basis. Coordination may be based on reciprocity or one-sided altruism. The aim of the interaction is not material gain but to help others. (Kornai, 1984).

Aggressive coordination: There is a hierarchical relationship between the superordinated and the subordinated actors. Participation is nonvoluntary. The superordinate uses force against the subordinate to achieve the desired transaction. (Kornai, 1984).

Kornai (1984) notes that in reality, the different coordination mechanisms operate side by side—i.e., combinations of coordination mechanisms occur. However, the combination of different mechanisms is usually not stable. Bureaucratic or aggressive coordination may crowd out market or ethical coordination. Also, market coordination may crowd out ethical coordination.

In the psychology literature, Ryan and Deci (2017) have illuminated the relationship between intrinsic and extrinsic motivation, i.e., motivation that is inherent to the task itself and motivation that relies on external rewards or sanctions. In the economic literature, the crowding-out effect, i.e., instances in which external rewards reduce the actor's internal motivation, has been explored both conceptually and through a number of experimental studies (Frey, 1997).

An instructive case is the experiment of the Haifa Daycare Center (Gnezzy & Rustichini, 2000). In the experiment, a fine was introduced to encourage parents to arrive on time to pick up their children. The result was disastrous. The number of late arrivals of parents doubled. After twelve weeks, the experimenters eliminated the fine, but—surprisingly—the higher level of tardiness of the parents persisted.

In analyzing the Haifa case, Bowles (2016) concluded that the counterproductive result suggests "a negative synergy between economic incentives and moral behavior. Placing a price on lateness (. . .) seems to have undermined the parents' sense of ethical obligation to avoid inconveniencing the teachers, leading them to think of lateness as just another commodity they could purchase" (Bowles, 2016: 4–5).

Another important experiment about the negative synergy between market incentives and ethical motivation was executed by Falk and Szech (2013). They demonstrated that using the market as a frame of reference in decision-making provides a good opportunity for people to morally disengage from considerations about doing harm to third parties. In the experiment, subjects chose between saving a mouse's life and receiving money. In a market setting, the willingness to kill the mouse was substantially higher than in the case of individual moral decision-making.

There are cases where ethical motivation and market incentives go hand in hand, creating positive synergy. The Home Kitchen Restaurant in London is such a case. In 2024, Michelin-starred chef Adam Simmonds opened a restaurant staffed by homeless people. He says that "Without a purpose, business is nothing." Home Kitchen pays its homeless employees above the living wage and aims to change public perceptions of homelessness (Cohen, 2024).

10.4 The Promise of the Civil Economy

The concept of the civil economy is traced to the Italian economist Antonio Genovesi (1713–1769), a contemporary of Adam Smith. He favored a different version of capitalism in which the principles of reciprocity, responsibility, and redistribution play a central role. Thanks to the dedicated work of Bruni and Zamagni (2007, 2016), the civil economy tradition has entered today's economic discourse about renewing capitalism and the market system.

Global financial capitalism has eroded the moral economy on which all economic transactions ultimately depend and is pushing a growth model that elevates profit above all else. The civil economy tradition locates well-being, virtues, and the common good alongside economic goals. The civil economy seeks to address social problems through the market while maximizing human values and minimizing government intervention. It is a distinct approach that offers individuals, corporations, and governments a framework for operating markets in a humane and socially accountable way (Bruni & Zamagni, 2016).

The civil economy model can be contrasted with the mainstream market economy model in different dimensions.

With the civil economy the ultimate goal of economic action is not pure profit-making but achieving public happiness, the basic strategy is not exploitation but sharing, the main organizing principle is not simple market exchange but mutual reciprocity, the governing form is not hierarchy but participation, the type of rationality is not efficiency but relationality, and the criterion of success is not financial wealth creation but creating value for all stakeholders (Table 10.1).

The civil economy tradition proposes that we develop economic arrangements that combine ethics and the market in a mutually supportive way. But acting according to a higher purpose should always precede self-interest in business and economic life if we are to benefit from ethical behavior and the market alike.

Table 10.1 Market economy versus civil economy

	Market economy	Civil economy
Ultimate goal	Profit-making	Public happiness
Basic strategy	Exploitation	Sharing
Organizing principle	Market exchange	Mutual reciprocity
Governing form	Hierarchy	Participation
Type of rationality	Efficiency	Relationality
Criterion of success	Financial wealth creation	Creating value for all stakeholders

Source Author's creation

References

BEC. (2025). https://www.businessethicscenter.com/. Accessed January 21, 2025.

Bouckaert, L., Ims, K. J. & Rona, P. (Eds.). (2018). *Art, spirituality and economics. Liber amicorum for laszlo zsolnai*. Springer.

Bowles, S. (2016). *The moral economy. Why good incentives are no substitute for good citizens*. Yale University Press.

Bruni, L. & Zamagni, S. (2007). *Civil Economy. Efficiency, equity, public Happiness*. Oxford, Peter Lang Academic Publishers.

Bruni, L. & Zamagni, S. (2016). *Civil economy: Another idea of the market*. Agenda Publishing.

Cohen, P. (2024). A fancy new restaurant in London, staffed by the recently homeless *TheNew York Times* October. 1, https://www.nytimes.com/2024/10/01/world/europe/restaurant-london-homeless.html. Accessed January 21, 2025.

Falk, A. & Szech, N. (2013). Morals and markets. *Science*, *340*, 707–711.

Frey, B. (1997). *Not Just for the money*. Edward Elgar.

Gnezzy, U. & Rustichini, A. (2000). A fine is a price. *The Journal of Legal Studies*, *29*(1), 1–17

Kornai, J. (1984). Bureaucratic and market coordination. *Osteuropa Wirtschaft*, *29*(4), 306–319.

Kornai, J. (1990). The affinity between ownership forms and coordination mechanisms. The common experience of reform in socialist countries. *Journal of Economic Perspectives*, *4*(3), 131–147.

Kornai, J. (1992). *The socialist system*. Princeton, Princeton & Oxford, Princeton University Press and Oxford University Press.

March, J. (2011). *Private email communication with Laszlo Zsolnai*. (February 26, 2011).

Musu, I. & Zamagni, S. (Eds.). (1990). *Social and ethical aspects of economics*. The Vatican City, Pontifical Council for Justice and Peace.

Musu, I. & Zamagni, S. (Eds.) (1993). *A közgazdaságtan társadalmi és etikai vetületei*. Budapest, Egyházfórum. (In Hungarian).

Petrini, C. & Padovani, G. (2005). *Slow food revolution. Da arcigola a terra madre. Una nuova cultura del cibo e della vita*. Rizzoli.

Ryan, R. M. & Deci, E. L. (2017). *Self-determination theory: Basic psychological needs in motivation, development, and wellness*. Guilford Publishing.

Shrivastava, P. & Zsolnai, L. (2022). Wellbeing oriented organizations: Connecting human flourishing with ecological regeneration. *Business Ethics, the Environment & Responsibility*, *31*(2), 386–397.

Smith, A. (1776). *An inquiry into the nature and causes of the wealth of nations, 1977*. The University of Chicago Press.

Tencati, A. & Zsolnai, L. (2012). Collaborative enterprise and sustainability: The case of slow food, *Journal of Business Ethics 68*(1), 35–52.

Zamagni, S. (2002). Humanizing the economy. In L. Zsolnai & W. Gasparski (Eds.), *Ethics and the future of capitalism* (pp. 89–110). Transaction Publishers.

Zamagni, S. (2005). A socio-economic reading of globalisation. *Society and Economy*, *25*(2), 181–205. https://doi.org/10.1556/socec.25.2003.2.6

Zamagni, S. (2006). Ethical anchoring of corporate social responsibility In L. Zsolnai (Ed.), *Interdisciplinary yearbook of business ethics* (pp. 31–50). Peter Lang Academic Publishers.

Zamagni, S. (2010). The cooperative as a collaborative enterprise. In A. Tencati & L. Zsolnai (Eds.), *The collaborative enterprise: Creating values for a sustainable world* (pp. 97–114). Peter Lang Academic Publishers.

Zamagni, S. (2011a). Avarice. In L. Bouckaert & L. Zsolnai (Eds.), *The Palgrave handbook of spirituality and business* (pp. 212–218). Palgrave Macmillan.

Zamagni, S. (2011b). Civil Economy. In L. Bouckaert & L. Zsolnai (Eds.), *The Palgrave handbook of spirituality and business* (pp. 277–284). Palgrave Macmillan.

Zamagni, S. (2017). Economics as if ethics mattered. In P. Rona & L. Zsolnai (Eds.), *Economics as a moral science* (pp. 21–41). Springer.

Zamagni, S. (2018). The idea of corporate social responsibility and the responses of economic theory. In L. Bouckaert, K. J. Ims, & P. Rona, P. (Eds.), *Art, spirituality and economics. Liber amicorum for Laszlo Zsolnai* (pp. 195–214), Springer.

Zsolnai, L. & Podmaniczky, L. (2010). Community supported agriculture. In A. Tencati & L. Zsolnai (Eds), *The collaborative enterprise: creating values for a sustainable world* (pp. 137–150). Peter Lang Academic Publishers.

Chapter 11
Value Creation in the Anthropocene

This chapter discusses the grand challenges of the Anthropocene era and shows the responsibility of business and other economic organizations in creating a devastating impact on the health of the planet. It suggests the concept of "sustainable value creation," understood as products, processes, organizations, and actions that satisfy real human needs and make positive impacts on nature, society, and future generations.

11.1 The Grand Challenges of the Anthropocene

Value creation in the Anthropocene must contend with balancing the well-being of humans with the well-being of other species, nature, and planetary ecosystems. The Anthropocene is characterized by the accelerating and devastating impacts of human economic, social, and cultural activities on Earth systems. With a global population of 8 billion, growing to 10 billion by mid-century, these impacts continue to breach planetary boundaries of life, are the root causes of climate change, and are driving the sixth mass extinction of species on earth (Rockström et al., 2009).

Human impacts implicate many practices of modern societies, but their central driver is the system of economic activities, economic value, and wealth creation. The global economy in its current extractive, polluting, consumerist, growth-oriented form needs fundamental rethinking. When we entered the Anthropocene era in the mid-1950s, the size of the global economy was under 10 trillion USD (as measured by GDP). By 2013, the global GDP had exceeded 100 trillion USD, a tenfold increase in production and consumption that is at the root cause of our current

---

This chapter is a slightly modified version of the previously published paper by Paul Shrivastava and the author: Shrivastava, P., & Zsolnai, L. (2023). Value Creation in the Anthropocene. In: Zsolnai, L., Walker, T., Shrivastava, P. (eds.) *Value Creation for a Sustainable World*, 3–18. Palgrave Macmillan, Cham. https://doi.org/10.1007/978-3-031-38016-7_1. Permission for reusing the paper is granted by Springer Nature.

© The Author(s), under exclusive license to Springer Nature Switzerland AG 2026
L. Zsolnai, *Planet Positive Economy*, Springer Studies in Alternative Economics,
https://doi.org/10.1007/978-3-032-21131-6_11

environmental crises. Earth systems have deteriorated at an accelerated pace as a result of this economic growth. We witnessed exponential increases in carbon dioxide, nitrous oxide, methane, stratospheric ozone, surface temperatures, ocean acidification, marine fish capture, shrimp aquaculture, coastal nitrogen, tropical forest loss, domesticated land, and biospheric degradation with consequent mass extinction of species (Steffen et al., 2015).

These impacts collectively are so dramatic that the continued functioning of Earth systems that have supported human civilizations in recent millennia is at risk. Moreover, while this growth benefitted many humans, it was also a source of tremendous economic inequalities both between nations and among people within nations (Piketty, 2015). This type of economic growth has led to a global economy in which 1% of the world's population owns 50% of its wealth. Additionally, by 2021, the collective global debt was $226 trillion USD, more than double the global GDP of $94 trillion USD. This means we are passing our debts to future generations. If we do not change our economic trajectory and the underlying business models, the clash between human activities and natural ecosystems will aggravate further, ending in the collapse of even more ecosystems. So, it is imperative that we find alternative modes of value creation that are both within the ecological limits of Earth systems and provide a just mode of functioning for all of Earth's inhabitants (Raworth, 2017).

One globally consensual approach towards sustainability is encapsulated in the UN Agenda 2030 and its sustainable development goals, agreed to by world leaders in 2015. But their implementation experience has identified many barriers and difficulties in executing integrated sustainable development at local and global levels (Stafford-Smith et al., 2016). The Sustainable Development Goals Report (2022) points out that cascading, interlinked crises have limited implementation of the goals and threaten the survival of humanity. The COVID-19 Pandemic pushed 93 million additional people into extreme poverty in 2020, resulting in a drop in immunization coverage and a rise in deaths from tuberculosis and malaria. 24 million learners—from pre-primary to university level—are at risk of never returning to school. 25% of the global population is now living in conflict zones. A record 100 million people have been forcibly displaced worldwide. Carbon emissions reduction commitments volunteered by nations will lead to a 14% increase in accumulated carbon by 2030, instead of a reduction by 43% necessary to limit global temperature rise to 2°C. Most national economies are facing record inflation, rising interest rates, and looming debt burdens. The polycrises of the Anthropocene pose special grand challenges from a research perspective and have been summarized by the Future Earth 2025 Vision (2014) document as follows:

1. Deliver water, energy, and food for all, and manage the synergies and trade-offs among them by understanding how these interactions are shaped by environmental, economic, social, and political changes.
2. Decarbonize socio-economic systems to stabilize the climate by promoting the technological, economic, social, political, and behavioral changes enabling transformations, while building knowledge about the impacts of climate change and adaptation responses for people and ecosystems.

3. Safeguard the terrestrial, freshwater, and marine natural assets underpinning human well-being by understanding relationships between biodiversity, ecosystem functioning, and services, and developing effective valuation and governance approaches.
4. Build healthy, resilient, and productive cities by identifying and shaping innovations that combine better urban environments and lives with declining resource footprints, and provide efficient services and infrastructures that are resilient to disasters.
5. Promote sustainable rural futures to feed rising and more affluent populations amidst changes in biodiversity, resources, and climate by analyzing alternative land uses, food systems, and ecosystem options, and identifying institutional and governance needs.
6. Improve human health by elucidating and finding responses to the complex interactions amongst environmental change, pollution, pathogens, disease vectors, ecosystem services, and people's livelihoods, nutrition, and well-being.
7. Encourage sustainable consumption and production patterns that are equitable by understanding the social and environmental impacts of consumption of all resources, opportunities for decoupling resource use from growth in well-being, and options for sustainable development pathways and related changes in human behavior.
8. Increase social resilience to future threats by building adaptive governance systems, developing early warning of global and connected thresholds and risks, and testing effective, accountable, and transparent institutions that promote transformations to sustainability.

At the core of addressing these challenges are the models and processes of economic value creation. We need new models of value creation and distribution, new models of doing business, and new models of economy at the regional, national, and international levels, so that we can ensure safe and just well-being for all of humanity, while ensuring the health of natural ecosystems that support life on Earth. This, in essence, is the path to a sustainable and equitable global economy of the future. To build such an economy, we need to begin by examining what sustainable and equitable value creation is. From our perspective, sustainability and equity go hand in hand, and involve both living within safe environmental boundaries and living with justice for all humans and other species.

11.2 Sustainable Value Creation

Business is the most powerful player in the Anthropocene and is mainly responsible for the degrading state of the biosphere in the last 50–60 years. Business-related activities, including material consumption, caused most of the negative effects in the biosphere.

The key problem is the nature, form, and scale of business operations. The working models of today's mainstream business organizations do not fit in the reality of the biosphere. Mainstream business models vary, but almost none of them are consistent with flourishing life on Earth (including human, nonhuman, and future life). To achieve meaningful change in the humanity-nature nexus, we have to reinvent the way business functions today. How can business become an ecologically conscious agent that operates within limits, that is, uses only its "fair earth share" and contributes to the flourishing of human and nonhuman life on Earth?

We suggest understanding sustainable value creation as products, processes, organizations, and actions that satisfy real human needs and make positive impacts on nature, society, and future generations. The most important features of sustainable value creation include (i) promoting frugality, (ii) acknowledging the intrinsic value of nature, (iii) producing negative emissions, and (iv) developing ecologically regenerative projects.

Frugality

Frugality implies organizing economic activities so that they use minimal material resources and produce minimal or even zero waste and negative impacts on the natural environment. Frugality is associated with a mindset and way of life that is characterized by voluntary simplicity, seeking sufficiency instead of efficiency (Bouckaert et al., 2008; Princen, 2005). It is a tendency to acquire goods and services in a restrained manner and the resourceful use of already owned economic goods and services to achieve a longer-term goal (Lastovicka et al., 1999).

Thoreau (1910) expressed a similar philosophy in his book *Walden*, with a zest for self-reliance and minimal possessions while living simply in nature. Deep ecology thinkers (Devall, 1988; Naess, 1989) formulated the principle of frugality as "Simple in means, rich in ends." Inspired by Buddhist philosophy, economist Schumacher (1973) urged us to achieve extraordinary results with small means.

Frugality appears as a precondition of human well-being. Psychological research shows that, contrary to the commonly held belief, materialistic value orientation undermines human well-being. Summarizing the main empirical findings, Kasser (2002) states, "People who are highly focused on materialistic values have lower personal wellbeing and psychological health than those who believe that materialistic pursuits are relatively unimportant. These relationships have been documented in samples of people ranging from the wealthy to the poor, from teenagers to the elderly, and from Australians to South Koreans" (Kasser 2022: 22).

Frugality is a rational strategy for individuals, organizations, communities, and nations, suggesting that they should reduce their material desires to a minimum. Above a certain "satisfying" level of material comfort, which includes enough food, clothing, shelter, and medicine, it is better not to cultivate but to reduce material desires. Producing and consuming less can bring major benefits for the person, for the community, and for nature as a whole (Zsolnai, 2017). Furthermore, frugality can be a design principle for building organizations and economies (Radjou, 2020; Shrivastava, 2015).

The Intrinsic Value of Nature

Today's mainstream economics fails to acknowledge the intrinsic value of nature. It evaluates environmental goods and services on the basis of a market value determined by competing economic actors. The value of the elements of nature is calculated by using the "willingness to pay" principle or shadow price techniques. But the value of natural entities cannot be calculated merely on the basis of their usefulness for humans. Market price is a poor and misleading model for assessing the value of natural entities. Gowdy and McDaniel (1995) demonstrated that the value of natural entities cannot be determined by the market mechanism.

To save the natural world, we need to accept the intrinsic value of nature. This means that natural creatures and natural ecosystems are valuable in and for themselves, not just in their usefulness for humans. This position is represented by different religious belief systems of humanity, including Indigenous world-views (Gottlieb, 1996) and various forms of environmental ethics (Brennan & Norva 2022).

In his encyclical *Laudato si'* Francis (2015) also urges us to acknowledge the intrinsic value of nature and organize our lives accordingly. The encyclical recalls that Jesus taught the attitude of admiration when "he invited us to contemplate the lilies of the field and the birds of the air" (Francis, 2015: §226).

Negative Emissions

The climate crisis is due to carbon emissions. Cumulating carbon is disturbing the carbon cycle that has remained stable over millions of years and has served to sustain life on Earth. Total carbon in the atmosphere from all human and nonhuman (natural) processes is now at 421 parts per million. This is vastly in excess of the 170 to 250 parts per million that have been stable for several million years. Much of the excess carbon accumulation is attributable to human activities involving fossil fuels since the 1750s, when coal emerged as a fuel. Even at the current level of carbon in the atmosphere, we have seen a 10°C rise in the global average temperature. Further carbon emissions and accumulation pose a very serious threat to global temperature and the climate system.

As per the global scientific and political consensus reflected in the 2015 Paris Climate Agreement, we must limit temperature rise to under 2°C (preferably under 1.5°C). This means that we need to reduce total carbon emissions now and in the coming decades. The global economy of the future will need to reverse the carbon emission trend. Economic activities will need to be designed not just to reduce carbon emissions but rather to remove carbon from the atmosphere and sequester it safely in ways that do not exacerbate climate change. The Drawdown Project (Hawken, 2017) lists a hundred different actions that can help draw carbon down from the earth's atmosphere.

Ecological Regeneration

Our current economies and economic concepts (that emerged in the eighteenth and nineteenth centuries) are premised on an unsustainable idea of endless extraction of value from the earth. First through agriculture, and later through mining extraction for industrial development, most economies are built on extractive principles. Economic value creation has been about using human ingenuity and technological innovations to extract materials from land, water, and atmosphere. Additional value is added in processing materials into finished products. Negative environmental impacts of this conversion are often externalized by organizations. The current model of the economy places limited and incomplete responsibilities for restoring any value or even removing pollution introduced in the production of economic value. This extractive approach to the economy was not seriously dysfunctional on a planetary scale in a world with a relatively small population (about 1.6 billion prior to 1900). But in a full world of 8 billion people that we face today, and with the population growing to 10 billion, this extractive approach is unsustainable. Earth systems are delicately balanced living ecosystems that can yield life sustenance to a certain degree and scale. Extraction beyond the carrying capacity of ecosystems leads to their collapse.

Future economic systems will need to be built on principles of ecological regeneration. Regeneration refers to the ability of an organism (cell, tissue, plant, forest, landscape) to recover from damage. At the ecosystem level, it is the capacity of the environment and its living populations to recover from damage. Economic systems designed on the principle of ecological regeneration can ensure restoration of the health and integrity of the ecosystems, even as they deliver economic benefits. Regenerative principles are now being applied to agriculture, mining, textiles, finance, and other industries (Cox et al., 2023; Lovins et al., 2018).

11.3 Cases of Sustainable Value Creation

We present and analyze value creation models from various parts of the world that serve human flourishing and ecological regeneration. Cases include Bodø as the Cultural Capital of Europe, Irish agricultural company Devenish, Danish renewable and green energy company Ørsted, the Chinese start-up and social movement Green Monday, the Jokkmokk's Market in Sweden, and Italian coffee producer illycaffé, Italian vegan fashion company Miomojo, place-based maker enterprises in Santa Fe (USA), Cumbria (UK), and the Yellow River Valley (China), open-source digital platform ENVIENTA, female Italian digital enterprise Veralab, and international NGO Health in Harmony which operates in Indonesia, Brazil, and Madagascar.

Jakobsen and Capra (2023) explored how challenges in the UN Sustainable Development Goals can be solved through a transdisciplinary approach. They synthesized principles and values inspired by "The Systems View of Life" (Capra & Luisi, 2014) and "Transformative Ecological Economics" (Jakobsen, 2017) for developing sustainable business models. They presented an outline of sustainable business models and discussed the problems of putting sustainable business models into practice using experiences from the project "Bodø as European Cultural Capital."

Donoghue and O'Higgins (2023) advocated that the implementation of the UN Sustainable Development Goals is a significant way of realizing the creation of value by business for a better and more sustainable world. They propose a virtuous cycle between Sustainable Development Goals implementation and the establishment of a social contract, enabled by trust. The paper provides some examples of value creation through the triad of Sustainable Development Goals implementation, the social contract, and trust.

Rendtorff (2023) analyzed the vision, mission, strategy, and production of the Danish renewable energy company Ørsted, which was transformed from being the Danish Oil and Natural Gas Company (DONG) to an offshore wind energy company relying entirely on producing renewable and green energy. He demonstrated that Ørsted implements values-driven management and Sustainable Development Goals in business practices. Ørsted relies on a strategy of transformation towards sustainability through a competitive business strategy of being the best energy provider through the production of green and renewable energy. The business model of Ørsted reveals how a progressive company can become a key contributor to sustainable development, zero-carbon emissions, and a future with control over climate change.

Ocsai (2023) reviewed the problems of food production in the Anthropocene and explored how a business enterprise could serve as a social movement and in what way these two could reinforce each other to reach sustainable value creation. This is illustrated by the case of Green Monday, a movement and a social start-up group of plant-based food in Hong Kong, which promotes low-carbon, sustainable lifestyles and strives for climate mitigation, food security, and animal welfare. Green Monday provides valuable insights into how collaborative actions of a social movement and a related business organization can help to meet real human needs and contribute to the preservation and regeneration of nature.

Sörensson (2023) discussed the role of local culture in creating sustainable value. She investigated a 400-year-old winter market in Jokkmokk, Sweden, to show how Indigenous people's culture affects the value of sustainability for tourists. She explored the role of culture in sustainability and value creation in the Winter Market. The result shows that the Sami culture constitutes the main value for visiting the place both during the Jokkmokk Winter Market and at other times of the year.

Ims and Zsolnai (2023) argued that the dominating conventional corporate model and global trade have created massive market-driven social changes globally, often characterized by the "race to the bottom," exploited vulnerable producers, reduced biodiversity, polluted environments, and led to dangerous climate change. They described the Fairtrade partnership model and compared it with the Bottom of the Pyramid model. Then they analyzed the case of illycaffé, an international company that sells coffee-related products in more than 130 countries. Illycaffé has developed a true partnership with local coffee producers that goes beyond Fairtrade because of its extraordinary focus on quality, care, and sustainability.

Rozsa (2023) warned that the ecological and social effects of the highly globalized fashion industry are increasingly destructive. Common industry practices are insensitive to ecological integrity, social justice, and animal welfare. The paper introduced the concept of vegan fashion and showed how Miomojo, an Italian fashion brand, reduces ecological destruction and the suffering of animals by applying the principles of veganism in fashion. This Bergamo-based company produces cruelty-free fashion products that exclude animal components. The paper showed the viability of this alternative business model to cope with the ethical and ecological challenges of the fashion industry.

Zhang et al. (2023) investigated place-based, maker enterprises that delineate their practices through the lens of sustainability and explored the potential of design to support their long-term development. They reported the results of field research in three distinct regions of the world: Santa Fe in the USA, which is renowned as a major center of traditional crafts; Cumbria in the UK, where a number of traditional but endangered craft enterprises are located; and the Yellow River Valley in China, where UNESCO's Intangible Cultural Heritage Convention plays a significant role in regional and national support of traditional practices. Key findings include the following: (i) connections to place and the values and motivations of the makers or enterprise owners, (ii) strong connections between craft-making practices and sustainability; (iii) a variety of business models to align the enterprise with sustainability; and (iv) potential opportunities for designers to contribute to maker enterprises. These findings can help to develop a practical location-making framework developed for supporting sustainable development in small-scale maker enterprises.

J. Veress (2023) analyzed a digital platform promoting "open source everything," including hardware. ENVIENTA Innovation Hub facilitates the amalgamation of global knowledge sharing with local provision of goods and services while minimizing the environmental footprint of producers, consumers, and innovators. Such cosmo-localization allows local economy development, which, by deploying digital technologies, enhances the autonomy of both communities and individuals. J. Veress (2023) stressed that the envisioned concept facilitates the localized fulfillment of genuine needs with personalized products and services, life quality improvements, environmental footprint reduction, and enhanced stewardship/caretaking toward nature. In the ENVIENTA model, the enhancement of mutual trust feeds the cooperative dynamics of the interactions and relationships that create interdependence and a non-zero-sum game approach.

Fioravante and Del Baldo (2023) addressed gender inequality as a lack of Integral Human Development. They connected Integral Human Development and feminist ethics to provide a model of intersectional organization in business. They used the case of female digital entrepreneur, Cristina Fogazzi, founder and owner of Veralab, who is successfully engaged in fighting against gender inequality through intersectional value creation. The case shows coherence between female inclusion and emancipation and the internal values of the organization.

T. Veress (2023) presented community economies and "growthism" as two radically different approaches to value creation and ways to organize economic activities. Growthism drives the institutionalization of privately appropriable rents and profit-generating arrangements, often with little regard to ecological sustainability and genuine human needs. Community economies' principles and models were illustrated with two case studies. One is Health in Harmony, an international NGO that operates health clinics in Indonesia, Brazil, and Madagascar with the aim of saving rainforests by helping local villagers to adopt livelihoods not dependent on illegal logging. The other case is the sustainable food network, a hypothetical system of organizations aiming to produce food through ecologically sustainable and socially just methods. T. Veress (2023) argued that community economies (i) favor the provisioning of genuine social needs instead of profit making, (ii) prefer resource sharing over commodification and enclosures, (iii) allow other-than-monetary ways for human interactions, (iv) cultivate participatory practices based on flat hierarchical relationships, (v) strive for material sufficiency, (vi) seek nonviolent technological solutions, and (vii) prefer common property ownership design. Community economies can be considered as autonomy-supporting social arrangements in which people can experience and practice a wide range of prosocial activities.

Prayukvong et al. (2023) analyzed the sufficiency economy philosophy formulated by the late Thai King Bhumibol Adulyadej. "Sufficiency" means balancing reasonable moderation in production against the need for protection from sudden internal and external shocks. The sufficiency economy philosophy follows the "Middle Path" as a guiding principle for all classes of society and government. Knowledge, thoughtfulness, prudence, and ethical integrity are essential to achieve it. Prayukvong et al. (2023) explored the use of Sufficiency Economy Philosophy as a method of social innovation for enhancing the delivery of public services and for localizing the process of sustainable development in three cases of local governments in Thailand. The first case shows how a local administration built a program to produce renewable energy (household cooking gas) from pig farm waste while earning revenue from carbon credits. The second case involves a local administration setting up a community welfare fund to reduce the inequality of people who have not received a basic income. Finally, the third case is about a local administration encouraging residents to build their own recycling project rather than waiting for top-down government action. Together, the cases show the potential of Sufficiency Economy Philosophy as a method of bottom-up social action for sustainable development.

References

Bouckaert, L., Opdebeeck, H., & Zsolnai, L. (Eds.). (2008). *Frugality: Rebalancing material and spiritual values in economic life*. Peter Lang Publishing.

Brennan, A. & Norva, Y. S. Lo. (2022). Environmental ethics. In *The Stanford Encyclopedia of Philosophy*. https://plato.stanford.edu/archives/sum2022/entries/ethics-environmental/. Accessed March 6, 2023.

Capra, F., & Luisi, P. L. (2014). *The systems view of life—A unifying vision*. Cambridge University Press.

Cox, D., White, C., & Bollier, D. (2023). *The great regeneration: Ecological agriculture, open-source technology, and a radical vision of hope*. Chelsea Green Publishing.

Devall, B. (1988). *Simple in means, rich in ends: Practicing deep ecology*. Gibbs Smith.

Donoghue, D., & O'Higgins, E. (2023). The United Nations Sustainable Development Goals—A pathway to value creation for a sustainable world. In L. Zsolnai, T. Walker, & P. Shrivastava (Eds.), *Value creation for a sustainable world: Innovating for ecological regeneration and human flourishing* (pp. 41–62). Palgrave-Macmillan.

Fioravante, V. R., & Del Baldo, M. (2023). Integral human development against gender inequality: Intersectional value creation. In L. Zsolnai, T. Walker, & P. Shrivastava (Eds.), *Value creation for a sustainable world: Innovating for ecological regeneration and human flourishing* (pp. 213–238). Palgrave-Macmillan.

Francis, P. (2015). Praised be: On the care of our common home. *Encyclical letter Laudatio SI' of the holy father Francis*. The Vatican City.

Future Earth 2025 Vision. (2014). https://futureearth.org/2014/11/06/future-earth-2025-vision-sets-the-framework-for-the-programmes-contribution-to-global-sustainable-development/. Accessed March 9, 2023.

Gottlieb, R. S. (Ed.). (1996). *This sacred earth. Religion, nature, environment*. Blackwell.

Gowdy, J., & McDaniel, C. N. (1995). One world, one experiment: Addressing the biodiversity–economics conflict. *Ecological Economics, 15*(3), 181–192.

Hawken, P. (2017). *Drawdown: The most comprehensive plan ever proposed to reverse global warming*. Penguin Books.

Ims, K., & Zsolnai, L. (2023). Fairtrade and Illycaffè. In L. Zsolnai, T. Walker, & P. Shrivastava (Eds.), *Value creation for a sustainable world: Innovating for ecological regeneration and human flourishing* (pp. 119–132). Palgrave-Macmillan.

Jakobsen, O. (2017). *Transformative ecological economics—Process philosophy, ideology and utopia*. Routledge.

Jakobsen, O., & Capra, F. (2023). The systems view of life and ecological economics for developing sustainable business models. In L. Zsolnai, T. Walker, & P. Shrivastava (Eds.), *Value creation for a sustainable world: Innovating for ecological regeneration and human flourishing* (pp. 21–39). Palgrave-Macmillan.

Kasser, T. (2002). *The high price of materialism*. MIT Press.

Lastovicka, J. L., Bettencourt, L. A., Hughner, R. S., & Kuntze, R. J. (1999). Lifestyle of the tight and frugal: Theory and measurement. *Journal of Consumer Research, 26*, 85–98.

Lovins, H. L., Wallis, S., Wijkman, A., Fullerton, J., & Raworth, K. (2018). *A finer future: Creating an economy in service to life*. New Society Publishers.

Naess, A. (1989). *Ecology, community and lifestyle. Outline of an ecosophy*. Cambridge University Press.

Ocsai, A. (2023). Sustainable value creation through business as a social movement: The case of Green Monday. In L. Zsolnai, T. Walker, & P. Shrivastava (Eds.), *Value creation for a sustainable world: Innovating for ecological regeneration and human flourishing* (pp. 81–102). Palgrave-Macmillan.

Piketty, T. (2015). *Capital in the twenty-first century*. Harvard University Press.

Prayukvong, W., Puntasen, A., & Hoopes, J. E. (2023). The sufficiency economy philosophy as an approach to social innovation: Case studies of local governments in Thailand. In L. Zsolnai, T. Walker, & P. Shrivastava (Eds.), *Value creation for a sustainable world: Innovating for ecological regeneration and human flourishing* (pp. 265–284). Palgrave-Macmillan.

Princen, T. (2005). *The logic of sufficiency*. MIT Press.

Radjou, N. (2020, August 6). The rising frugal economy. *Sloan Management Review*, https://sloanreview.mit.edu/article/the-rising-frugal-economy/. Accessed December 9, 2025.

Raworth, K. (2017). *Doughnut economics: Seven ways to think like a 21st-century economist*. Random House.

Rendtorff, J. D. (2023). Sustainable solutions to the global climate problem: The case of the renewable and green energy company ørsted. In L. Zsolnai, T. Walker, & P. Shrivastava (Eds.), *Value creation for a sustainable world: Innovating for ecological regeneration and human flourishing* (pp. 63–80). Palgrave-Macmillan.

Rockström, J., Steffen, W., Noone, K., Persson, Å., F. S. Chapin III, E. F. L., Lenton, T. M., Scheffer, M., Folke, C., Schellnhuber, J., Nykvist, B., de Wit, C. A., Hughes, T., van der Leeuw, S., Rodhe, H., Sörlin, S., Snyder, P. K., Costanza, R., Svedin, U., Falkenmark, M., … Foley, J. (2009). A safe operating space for humanity. *Nature*, *461*, 472–475.

Rozsa, Z. (2023). Vegan fashion: The case of Miomojo. In L. Zsolnai, T. Walker, & P. Shrivastava (Eds.), *Value creation for a sustainable world: Innovating for ecological regeneration and human flourishing* (pp. 133–152). Palgrave-Macmillan.

Schumacher, E. F. (1973). *Small is beautiful. Economics as if people mattered*. Abacus.

Shrivastava, P. (2015). Organizational sustainability under degrowth. *Management Research Review*, *38*(6). https://doi.org/10.1108/MRR-07-2014-0157

Sörensson, A. (2023). The role of sami culture in creating sustainable cultural value for tourists: A case study of Jokkmokk's winter market. In L. Zsolnai, T. Walker, & P. Shrivastava (Eds.), *Value creation for a sustainable world: Innovating for ecological regeneration and human flourishing* (pp. 103–117). Palgrave-Macmillan.

Stafford-Smith, M., Griggs, D., Gaffney, O., Ullah, F., Reyers, B., Kanie, N., Stigson, B., Shrivastava, P., Leach, M., & O'Connell, D. (2016). Integration: The key to implementing the Sustainable Development Goals. *Sustainability Science*, *12*, 911–919. https://doi.org/10.1007/s11625-016-0383-3

Steffen, W., Broadgate, W., Deutsch, L., Gaffney, O., & Ludwig, C. (2015). The trajectory of the Anthropocene: The great acceleration. *Anthropocene Review*, *2*, 81–98. https://doi.org/10.1177/2053019614564785

Sustainable Development Goals Report. (2022). https://www.un.org/sustainabledevelopment/progress-report/. Accessed March 9, 2023.

Thoreau, H. D. (1910). *Walden*. T. Y. Crowell & Co.

Veress, J. (2023). Digitalization and social innovation—The case of ENVIENTA. In L. Zsolnai, T. Walker, & P. Shrivastava (Eds.), *Value creation for a sustainable world: Innovating for ecological regeneration and human flourishing* (pp. 187–211). Palgrave-Macmillan.

Veress, T. (2023). Principles and models of community economies. In L. Zsolnai, T. Walker, & P. Shrivastava (Eds.), *Value creation for a sustainable world: Innovating for ecological regeneration and human flourishing* (pp. 239–262). Palgrave-Macmillan.

Zhang, W., Walker, S., Evans, M., & Humphreys, P. (2023). The located-making framework for sustainable enterprise. In L. Zsolnai, T. Walker, & P. Shrivastava (Eds.), *Value creation for a sustainable world: Innovating for ecological regeneration and human flourishing* (pp. 153–186). Palgrave-Macmillan.

Zsolnai, L. (2017). Frugality and the intrinsic value of nature. In O. Jakobsen & L. Zsolnai (Eds.), *Integral ecology and sustainable business* (pp. 67–76).

References

Chapter 12
Well-Being Policies for Countries and Cities

Today, most countries and cities follow policies that strive for competitiveness, economic growth, and wealth creation. However, this uncritical pursuit of mainstream economic dictates is producing considerable "ills" in the Anthropocene, including climate change, biodiversity loss, ecosystem collapse, and national and global inequalities. This chapter presents some leading alternative approaches by countries and cities that focus on creating well-being in a broad socioecological context. The emerging well-being-focused policy framework includes the Gross National Happiness of Bhutan, Costa Rica's National Decarbonization Plan, the Well-being budget of New Zealand, and the "doughnut economy" of Amsterdam. The well-being policy framework abandons the idea of gross domestic product (GDP)-centered economic growth and directly targets human well-being and ecological regeneration. It implies encouraging economic and business activities and programs that create socioecological well-being, and discouraging or even punishing activities and programs that create ill-being for people and the Earth.

12.1 The Problem: Economic Growth and Wealth Creation

The current era of capitalism is associated with two basic challenges that suggest consideration of the need for economics to be refocused on wellbeing. First, mainstream businesses and markets generate enormous financial and material wealth, but they also, unintentionally, create risks and ecological destruction.

This chapter is a slightly modified version of the previously published paper by the author and Andras Ocsai, Gabor Kovacs, Kalman Kelemen and Zoltan Valcsicsak: Zsolnai, L., Ocsai, A., Kovacs, G., Kelemen, K., Valcsicsak, Z. (2023). Wellbeing Policies for Countries and Cities. In: Zsolnai, L., Walker, T., Shrivastava, P. (eds.) *Value Creation for a Sustainable World*, 285–307. Palgrave Macmillan, Cham. https://doi.org/10.1007/978-3-031-38016-7_14. The paper is used by the permission of Springer Nature.

© The Author(s), under exclusive license to Springer Nature Switzerland AG 2026
L. Zsolnai, *Planet Positive Economy*, Springer Studies in Alternative Economics,
https://doi.org/10.1007/978-3-032-21131-6_12

Post-1950s, a great acceleration of ecological degradation occurred, commensurate with an increasing population and related economic and social activity (Steffen et al., 2015). The extent of the respective changes to ecosystems is causing climate change, reducing biodiversity, and threatening to exceed several "planetary boundaries" (Rockström et al., 2009). Second, current business and market mechanisms have, over the past century, led to the creation of extreme inequality in wealth and income distribution (Piketty, 2015). Mainstream businesses and markets deliberately skew the distribution of wealth in favor of investors and those who are already wealthy, causing profound and unsustainable inequalities in society (Shrivastava & Zsolnai, 2022). While the world economy has continued to grow over the past half-century, this has led to the bifurcation of society, with the result that less than 1% of the population now controls the majority (over 50%) of the world's wealth. In light of these trends, we need an anchoring concept that can ensure the well-being of the population of 10 billion that is expected to inhabit the earth by 2050. Universal well-being may be the concept that is responsive to the key challenges of the Anthropocene (climate change, biodiversity loss, and rising inequality).

Mainstream economics holds that the ultimate goal of the economic system is growth measured by GDP, and the main function of economic policy is to foster this economic growth. GDP is a monetary measure of the market value of all the final goods and services produced in a specific period by national economies.

Another problem with economic growth policies is that they do not take into account the harm caused to the natural environment. Also, GDP does not capture the state of human health and the level of education in society (Dréze & Sen, 2013). Similarly, GDP does not include the value of household and other unpaid work (Nussbaum, 2013).

Since the publication of the *Limits to Growth* report of the Club of Rome (Meadows et al., 1972), there have been many criticisms of unlimited economic growth and growth-oriented economic policies. Ecological critiques include the claim that infinite economic growth is not possible in a finite environment, such as the Earth (Daly, 1996, 2007). Social critiques include the claim that economic growth necessarily produces inequality within societies and globally. Further, psychological studies show that above a certain level of development, economic growth does not contribute to the happiness and well-being of people but actually decreases it (Easterlin, 2005).

The Happy Planet (2019) measures the sustainable well-being of countries. The index multiplies subjective life satisfaction by life expectancy at birth then, divides that by the ecological footprint (the amount of land required per person to sustain a country's consumption over time). Costa Rica, Vanuatu, Colombia, Switzerland, and Ecuador score highest on sustainable wellbeing. However, the results show that none of today's economies can meet the criteria of providing well-being for all people and functioning in an ecologically sustainable way (See Table 12.1).

Table 12.1 Top-scoring countries on the Happy Planet Index in 2019

Country	Happy planet score	Life expectancy	Life satisfaction	Ecological footprint
Costa Rica	62.1	+	+	–
Vanuatu	60.4	–	+	–
Colombia	60.2	+	+	–
Switzerland	60.1	+	+	– –
Ecuador	58.8	+	–	+

+ indicates good performance, – indicates underperformance, and – – indicates strong underperformance
Source Authors' construction based on Happy Planet Index (2019)

12.2 Well-Being Economics

It is no surprise that novel approaches suggest abandoning policies that strive for economic growth. No-growth theories suggest that ecological sustainability and social well-being can only be achieved if economies change their development trajectories.

American ecological economist Herman Daly (1996, 2007) forcefully criticized modern growth economics. He claimed that the present trajectory of economic growth is "uneconomic" in many countries because it makes individuals poorer, not richer. Instead, Daly favored a steady-state economy where the stock of physical wealth and the population size are constant. In effect, such an economy does not grow over time.

In an influential book, *Prosperity without Growth,* British economist Jackson (2009) argues for a sustainable economy. Based on empirical evidence, he states that beyond a certain point, economic growth does not increase human well-being. Jackson argues that our current economic growth models are not sustainable as they strain our planet's resources to breaking point and cause climate change, environmental damage, and psychological harm. He shows the possibility and the necessity of postgrowth economic policies that increase widespread prosperity without economic growth.

French economist and philosopher Serge Latouche (2010) argued for rethinking the basic idea that our societies should be based on growth. He offered a radical alternative to economic growth—namely, "de-growth." Latouche suggested that while many realize that the never-ending pursuit of growth is incompatible with a finite planet, we must recognize the implications of this. We need to produce less and consume less. If we do not change course, ecological and human disasters will occur.

Oxford-based economist Raworth (2017) developed the so-called "doughnut economy" model, which consists of two concentric rings: a social foundation to ensure that no one falls short of life's essentials and an ecological ceiling to ensure that humanity does not collectively overshoot the planetary boundaries that protect

Earth's life-supporting systems. Cities including Amsterdam, Brussels, Copenhagen, Berlin, and Cambridge are experimenting with Raworth's doughnut model in their efforts to tackle the climate crisis and ecological collapse.

Well-being reflects the convergence of good human life (physical, mental, and spiritual), equity and fairness, a peaceful community, and supporting social relationships within a flourishing natural environment (Shrivastava & Zsolnai, 2022). A well-being economy is scaled to remain within planetary biophysical boundaries and the capacity of local ecological life support systems to meet human needs. It is designed to supply the human needs for food, water, health, education, shelter, energy, dignity, security, voice, and purpose (Costanza, 2018). A principal value of the well-being economy is equity and fairness in the distribution of resources, income, and wealth. Collective flourishing requires the efficient allocation of common ecological and social capital, the goal of a well-being economy. Such an economic approach incorporates governance and institutions that are fair, responsive, just, and accountable (Costanza et al., 2020).

Utility or profit is a one-dimensional outcome, but well-being can be represented as a multicomponent vector that contains material and nonmaterial elements. Various stocks and flows together determine how human and nonhuman being's flourish. Chilean economist Max-Neef (1989) developed a matrix of needs and satisfiers that shows the manifold aspects of human wellbeing. The matrix contains existential needs ("being," "having," "doing," and "interacting") and axiological needs ("subsistence," "protection," "affection," "understanding," "participation," and "idleness") and classifies dozens of corresponding satisfiers.

Positive psychology and happiness studies reveal that material and nonmaterial factors contribute to one's well-being or ill-being. Utility is a poor and incomplete measure of how well a person is functioning. Similarly, psychologists identified several strategies by which people can systematically undermine and destroy their own well-being and the well-being of others. Certainly, satisfaction of current preferences may have disastrous consequences for the persons involved (Skidelsky & Skidelsky, 2012).

In modern economies, the role of economic policy is much more complex than using standard policy toolboxes such as taxes and subsidies, government regulations, quotas, remuneration schemes, and other monetary incentives.

An enabling mechanism associated with the well-being economy is the system of measurement and accounting. Well-being is not identical to aggregate income or wealth measured in Gross Domestic Product (GDP) or Gross National Product (GNP). Today, more holistic measures of economic performance have already been developed. Among them are the Genuine Progress Indicator (GPI), the Human Development Index, and the Organisation for Economic Co-operation and Development (OECD) Better Life Index (BLI).

The Genuine Progress Indicator (GPI) is a single-value measure that expands on GDP by adding in the value of nonmarket benefits (e.g., child-rearing and leisure) and subtracting the value of nonmarket costs (e.g., environmental degradation and the depletion of natural capital). It also adjusts for inequality across the population (Kubiszewski et al., 2013).

The Human Development Index (2022) is a summary indicator of average achievement in key dimensions such as a long and healthy life, being knowledgeable, and having a decent standard of living. The health dimension is assessed by life expectancy at birth; the education dimension is measured by the mean years of schooling for adults aged 25 years and older and expected years of schooling for children of school-starting age. Finally, the standard of living dimension is measured by GNP per capita. The Human Development Index is the geometric mean of normalized indices for each of the three dimensions.

The OECD Better Life Index (BLI) uses a dashboard of indicators: income, jobs, community, education, housing, environment, governance, health, life satisfaction, safety, and work-life balance. It is based on surveys that ask people's perceptions about their lives, health, and government (OECD, 2025).

These developments suggest that the primary function of economic policy is to enable well-being creation, and the performance of the economy should be evaluated in relation to the overall well-being of nature and society, which is how the economy serves the flourishing of life on Earth (human and nonhuman, present and future).

12.3 Well-Being Focused Countries and Cities

Well-being-focused policy frameworks are practiced in countries like Bhutan, Costa Rica, and New Zealand, and in cities like Amsterdam in the Netherlands. These new policy frameworks abandon the idea of GDP-centered economic growth and directly target human well-being and ecological regeneration. They encourage business and social activities and programs that create socioecological well-being and discourage or even punish those activities and programs that create ill-being for humans and nature.

Gross National Happiness of Bhutan

The approach and principles of creating genuine well-being and progress have been successfully applied in the Himalayan Kingdom of Bhutan through the country's unique holistic development model called "Gross National Happiness" (GNH). The GNH model has been the basis for the gradual and careful opening, modernization, and economic and social development of Bhutan, with its Buddhist culture, since the 1980s, with a strong emphasis on centuries-old traditions and the preservation of the natural environment. The birth of the concept of GNH can be traced back to King Jigme Singye Wangchuck, who believed that his country's own traditional values and the dominant principles of the global economic and political system could only be reconciled within a comprehensive development framework based on Buddhist spiritual values, long-term holistic sustainability, emphasis on the preservation of the natural environment and local culture, and a focus on economic management that goes beyond GDP-centered solutions (Valcsicsák, 2015).

Over the past decades, as the primary institutions of constitutional monarchy and parliamentary democracy have been built up in Bhutan, GNH has gradually been institutionalized. It has been given a scientific and professional background with the involvement of foreign experts and has been integrated into the country's administration. The first Bhutanese constitution, adopted in 2008, refers to it as a guiding goal for development and an important public policy-making tool of the government. In 2012, at the initiative of Bhutan, the UN organized a high-level meeting entitled "Wellbeing and happiness: defining a new economic paradigm," which encouraged member states to introduce alternative measures for including happiness in public policy goals. The first *World Happiness Report*, published for the meeting, provides a detailed description of the origins and cultural and historical embeddedness of GNH and how the concept is being put into practice (Ura et al., 2012).

The model of GNH is based on four pillars, which are (i) equitable and sustainable socioeconomic development, (ii) the preservation and promotion of culture, (iii) environmental conservation, and (iv) good governance.

The achievement of these four pillars is measured and assessed in nine dimensions, which are: (i) the psychological well-being of citizens (which includes life satisfaction, emotional balance, and the experience of spirituality); (ii) physical and mental health; (iii) participation in the education system; (iv) cultural knowledge and participation in cultural life; (v) personal time management (including work/rest balance); (vi) good governance (which includes political participation, access to essential services, and government performance); (vii) small community and family vitality; (viii) the impact and changes in the natural and urban environment; and (ix) living standards (which includes income, assets, and housing conditions) (Centre for Bhutan Studies & GNH Research, 2016; Kovacs, 2016). (See Fig. 12.1).

In the early 2000s, the Centre for Bhutan and GNH Studies designed a measurement system to quantify GNH and track changes in the GNH index over time. The metrics they have created convert the results of a questionnaire-based GNH survey of the population, carried out at intervals, into a number between "0" and "1" (the GNH Index for the period). The measurement of GNH incorporates both subjective and objective factors and examines what both modern science and Buddhism consider to be the essential conditions for human happiness (Ura et al., 2012).

GNH surveys were conducted in Bhutan in 2010 and 2015 on a representative sample. Data were collected by assigning 8 subjective and 25 objective indicators (33 in total) with 124 variables in nine dimensions. The GNH index uses a dual threshold (cutoff) method. Each indicator is assigned a sufficiency threshold, which indicates the level above which the individual being surveyed can be considered happy with respect to that indicator. The cross-dimensional happiness threshold indicates the proportion of sufficiency thresholds that the individual has to cross to be considered happy overall (Ura et al., 2012).

The country's GNH index increased from 0.743 in 2010 to 0.756 in 2015. In the GNH survey in 2015, 91.2% of the 7153 respondents were at least somewhat happy, and 43.4% were deeply happy. The application of GNH aims to inform

Fig. 12.1 Dimensions of gross national happiness. *Source* Authors' own elaboration

public policymaking to create economic and social conditions that help more people who are not at all happy to become happier (Centre for Bhutan Studies & GNH Research, 2016).

The government of Bhutan includes GNH indicators in its 5 year national planning. It uses GNH policy screening tools for vetting policies. Current Five-year plans use 16 key baseline indicators, primarily to track changes in ecology, culture, socioeconomy, and good governance (Ura, 2015).

GNH is a macrolevel, multidimensional, values-based approach that focuses on long-term, sustainable, and harmonious economic and social development while emphasizing the importance of preserving the mental balance of individuals, spiritual traditions, and the natural environment. It builds on values found in Buddhism, such as interconnectedness and compassion, responsibility for the community and nature, moderation, mindfulness, balance, and reducing the suffering of sentient beings.

National Decarbonization in Costa Rica

Costa Rica continuously outperforms Western countries on the Happy Planet Index (HPI) (Abdallah et al., 2021) and excels in human development relative to other countries with a similar level of income (Saborío et al., 2019).

Costa Rica is located in Central America, between Nicaragua and Panama. It has fewer than five million inhabitants. One-quarter of the country's territory is under official protection as a national park or biological reserve (Goehl, 1996), and it shelters about 5% of the known biodiversity in the world (Weil, 2007). The country is recognized as a natural paradise (Montmagny Grenier, 2020).

Following the civil war in 1948, the Costa Rican government adopted a progressive constitution that allowed the country to pursue a unique social and environmental development path (Helmuth, 2000; Saborío et al., 2019) by expanding military expenses on education, health care, and environmental conservation (Goehl, 1996). As a result, compared to other developing countries, Costa Rica's public education system is associated with a high literacy rate (Porter, 2019), and its healthcare system creates a long average life expectancy (Saborío et al., 2019). In addition, investment in natural capital contributed to the success story of ecotourism in Costa Rica as early as the late 1980s, with great emphasis on its characterization as a "green country" as a differentiating factor in the tourism industry (Government of Costa Rica, 2019; Dominguez, 2018; Miller, 2012; Horton, 2009).

By the early 1980s, Costa Rica had the highest rate of deforestation in Latin America (Honey, 2008). In response to this, the country implemented a progressive forest law in the mid-1990s and introduced its pioneering payments for environmental services (PES) program, thereby establishing a financial mechanism that promotes forest ecosystem conservation and combats land degradation. PES is a country-wide program that involves charging the users of environmental services for the services they receive. Landowners with sustainable forest management plans can participate in the program and receive direct payments for the environmental services that their lands produce if they adopt sustainable land use and forest-management techniques. The program is funded through Costa Rica's fuel tax and water charge (Pagiola, 2008; United Nations Climate Change, n.d.). Because of PES, deforestation in Costa Rica reversed in the early 2000s (Pagiola, 2008), and according to Barton (2013), because of the program, forest cover has now increased to more than 50% of the country's territory.

Costa Rica is also famous for its simple yet happy, relational lifestyle—referred to as *pura vida* (Wellbeing Economy Alliance, n.d.), which means "pure life." The deeper meaning refers to cultural identity and a national ethos dedicated to the enjoyment of the Costa Rican lifestyle (Weil, 2007). Pura vida embodies the deep interconnectedness of the Costa Rican communities (Dominguez, 2018). This also influences the country's development strategy, which is aimed at decarbonizing the entire economy by 2050 (Government of Costa Rica, 2019).

In his inaugural speech in 2018, President Carlos Alvarado expressed the country's aspiration to become decarbonized and resilient. In line with its strategic goals, Costa Rica published a National Decarbonization Plan, through which the country aspires to create a green, resilient, and equitable economy without emissions. The focal areas of decarbonization are (i) transport and sustainable mobility, (ii) energy use, green buildings and industry, (iii) integrated waste management, and (iv) agriculture, land use change, and nature-based solutions. In addition, the plan recognizes eight institutional requirements for transformation (so-called cross-cutting strategies), which are (i) the comprehensive reform of institutionality, (ii) a green tax reform, (iii) funding strategies and investment attraction for transformation, (iv) digitalization and a knowledge-based economic strategy, (v) labor strategies for a "just transition," (vi) inclusion, human rights and the promotion of gender equality, (vii) transparency, and an open data strategy, and (viii) an educational and cultural strategy for a fossil-fuel-free Costa Rica. Decarbonization and resilience are recognized as the means of transforming the current economic development model into an inclusive economy that enhances the well-being of all citizens (Government of Costa Rica, 2019).

The Well-being Budget of New Zealand

New Zealand is known for its pristine wilderness and the unique culture of the Māori people, who initially settled in the country's islands around seven centuries ago. New Zealand is now among the most developed countries in the world (Blyth et al., 2022). However, the price of economic development has been growing social difficulties and the degradation of the natural environment.

New Zealand performs well on numerous measures of well-being relative to most countries, but it is among the worst, for instance, for family and sexual violence, affordable rental housing, well-being, and income for minority society (Māori), and child well-being and poverty. In 2020, more than 210,000 children were living in poverty (18.4%), and the suicide rate of young people has been among the highest in the OECD (GoNZ, 2020; Jaquiery, 2022). Ecological harm, to a considerable extent, has been due to economic growth. The country was one of the worst performers in terms of growth in emissions, as the latter grew by 57% between 1990 and 2018 (McClure, 2021).

In 2017, New Zealand took an extraordinary step when it passed a groundbreaking law granting personhood status to the Whanganui River, revered as sacred by the Māori people (Fig. 12.2). The law declares that the river is a living whole, from the mountains to the sea, incorporating all its physical and metaphysical elements. The river is represented by officials, one from the crown and one from the Māori community, who have been provided with NZ$80 million as financial redress and a NZ$30 million fund for restoring the river's health (Davison, 2017).

In early 2019, Prime Minister Jacinda Ardern declared that short-term political thinking must be replaced by the concept of "environmental stewardship" derived from the ancient Māori philosophy, and that the state budget should be based on empathy, kindness, and altruism to improve people's quality of life (Makortoff, 2019; Parker, 2019). Later in 2019, New Zealand's government announced the world-first "wellbeing" budget aimed at tackling the social and environmental challenges of the country (WEA, 2019; GoNZ, 2020).

The main goals of Jacinda Ardern's government were to ensure the well-being of everyone and take effective action against climate change. The Well-being Budget of New Zealand created a holistic framework that focused on priorities that broaden how New Zealand defines its success, including reporting in line with a more comprehensive set of well-being indicators. This incorporates not only the health of the economy but also the health of natural resources, people, and communities, and allocated billions of NZ$ to achieve measurable results (WEA, 2019; GoNZ, 2020; Jaquiery, 2022).

Fig. 12.2 The Whanganui River. *Source* http://en.wikipedia.org/wiki/Image:Whanganui_River.jpg licensed under the creative commons attribution-share alike 4.0 international

The priority areas on which the well-being budget focused were the following.

Taking Mental Health Seriously: New Zealand intends to support mental well-being for all New Zealanders, with particular focus on under-24 year-olds. A new front-line service for mental health programs provided access to 325,000 people by 2023/24.

Improving Child Well-being: the country is striving to reduce child poverty and child ill-being, including eliminating family violence. Specialist services were introduced to address family and sexual violence.

Supporting Māori and Pasifika Aspirations: the budget assisted with increasing Māori and Pacific incomes, skills, and opportunities—an additional 2,200 young people were included in the Pacific Employment Support Service.

Building a Productive Nation: In the digital age, the thriving of the whole nation is to be supported through innovation and social and economic opportunities. Bridging the venture capital gap so start-ups can grow and succeed was a goal.

Transforming the Economy: creating opportunities for productive businesses, regions, iwi (the largest social unit in Māori society), and others to transition to a sustainable and low-emissions economy. Encouraging sustainable land use (GoNZ, 2020).

In 2022, New Zealand published its first National Well-being Report. The report finds that well-being is improving in terms of income, health, life satisfaction, social cohesion, and trust. However, in other areas such as housing, education, mental health, risks associated with climate change, and other natural shocks, the country is still underperforming, especially since young generations are hit hard.

This clearly shows that for improving the well-being of New Zealanders, the systemic and long-standing challenges of intergenerational inequity and transitioning to a low-carbon and resilient economy should be tackled while prioritizing dignity, purpose, ecology, fairness, and participation (GoNZ, 2022; WEA, 2022).

Amsterdam's "Doughnut Economy"

The city of Amsterdam, known by many as the home of the painters Rembrandt and Van Gogh, celebrated its 750th "birthday" in 2025. Over the centuries, the once small fishing village became the most populous city in the Netherlands and one of the world's most important centers for finance, business, culture, and art. Having a long tradition of openness, liberalism, tolerance, and innovation, Amsterdam is now trying to become an inspirational example of twenty-first-century transformation in action (Bloomberg, 2018, DEAL, 2020).

In 2018, Femke Halsema was appointed Mayor of Amsterdam, and the coalition city government agreed on a plan entitled "A new spring and a new voice" to assist in the practical implementation of action centered on six main ambitions. Based on the principles of openness, transparency, and inclusivity, Amsterdam aimed to (i) promote equal opportunities and offer support to those who need it most; (ii) develop an open and tolerant city; (iii) build pleasant neighborhoods and a livable city; (iv) ensure the right to freedom and safety; (v) transform into a healthy and sustainable city; and (vi) improve democratic participation through offering everyone accessible digital services (CoA, 2019).

To help meet its goals and cope with the challenges caused by the worsening ecological crisis and the coronavirus pandemic, Amsterdam called on the "doughnut economy model" (Fig. 12.3). The concept was developed by Oxford economist Kate Raworth, who argues that humanity's activities should be conducted within an ecologically safe and socially just space (the "doughnut") where human and planetary well-being is balanced (Raworth, 2017; Boffey, 2020; Nugent, 2021).

Based on the United Nations' Sustainable Development Goals, the inner ring of the model includes the minimum social requirements for a "good life," or the social foundation. Shortfalls in this area in adequate food, health, education, income and work, peace and justice, political voice, social equity, gender equality, housing, energy, and safe water create deprivation for humanity. The outer ring of the doughnut designates the ecological ceiling defined by the nine planetary boundaries, as specified by Rockström and colleagues (2009). Ecological overshoot means that humanity is transgressing planetary boundaries and damaging climate, oceans, freshwater, soil, abundant biodiversity, air, and the ozone layer, or radically changing natural nitrogen and phosphorus cycles and excessively emitting artificial chemical pollutants (Raworth, 2017; Nugent, 2021).

Amsterdam formally embraced doughnut economics to support public policy decisions in April 2020—the first city in the world to do so. Initially, it served as a tool for guiding the city's social and economic recovery from the COVID-19 pandemic. Through intensive collaboration with civil society, city officials started to apply this approach to help implement their most ambitious initiative of

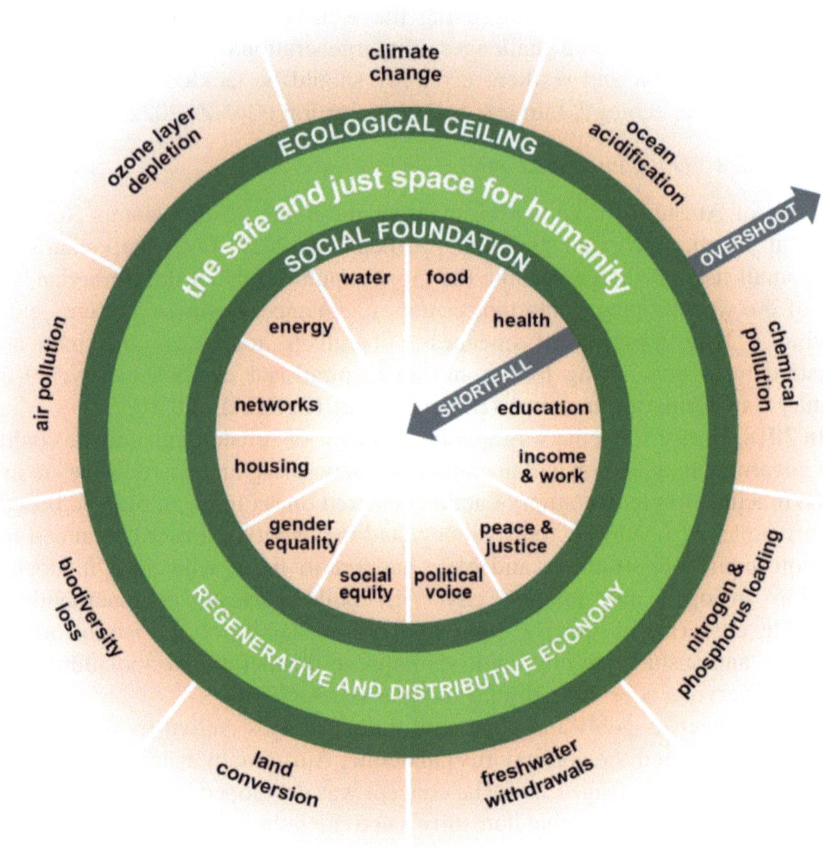

Fig. 12.3 The doughnut economy model. *Source* https://commons.m.wikimedia.org/wiki/File:Doughnut_(economic_model).jpg#mw-jump-to-license licensed under the creative commons attribution-share alike 4.0 international

developing a 100% circular economy by 2050. This is a holistic snapshot of Amsterdam's complex interconnections with the world in which it is embedded, which involves consideration of its local aspirations (thriving of people and place) and global social and ecological responsibilities (DEAL, 2020).

From an analysis of Amsterdam's own "doughnut" and the economic difficulties caused by the pandemic, adequate housing for citizens seemed to be one of the most pressing problems. Almost 20% of city tenants were unable to cover their basic needs after paying their rent, and just 12% of about 60,000 online applicants for social housing were successful. In parallel, environmental limits have been violated at many points, such as with the increase in carbon dioxide emissions, air pollution, excessive land use and fertilization, overfishing, and wastage of drinking water (Boffey, 2020).

By 2030, Amsterdam aims to be completely emissions-free; this will involve cutting the raw materials it needs to operate by half, allowing only electric vehicles, and using solar and wind sources to generate 80% of the electricity used by households. To improve air quality, the city will replace natural gas with renewable energy by 2040. The city plans to decrease carbon dioxide emissions by 55% by 2030 and by 95% by 2050 compared to the level of 1990. Amsterdam is determined to achieve climate neutrality and promote adaptability, use all suitable rooftops as solar power plants, and become a fully "circular city" by 2050 (CoA, 2022).

12.4 Conclusions

The examples of GNH of Bhutan, Costa Rica's National Decarbonization, the Well-being Budget of New Zealand, and the "doughnut economy" of Amsterdam represent novel approaches to and working models of well-being policies.

Bhutan, Costa Rica, New Zealand, and Amsterdam have special socioeconomic histories and unique "indigenous" cultures. Nevertheless, their well-being policies and models are deeply rooted in their histories and cultures, so these practices cannot be exported to other places without modifications. Instead, they represent "meta-models" that suggest usable guiding principles and values for creating appropriate policy frameworks in different contexts.

Scale is a critical issue. Bhutan, Costa Rica, and New Zealand are smaller and isolated countries. The question is whether a well-being framework can work in large countries or even medium-sized ones. Another question is how the notions of well-being can be adjusted or modified to apply to the political-economic complexity and value diversity of large and medium-sized countries.

The example of Amsterdam is instructive because it is a large, modern city. Its embrace of doughnut economics implies a progressive social movement that supports vulnerable segments of society. The city's climate action plan is ambitious. First, however, changes in policy direction must be institutionalized in terms of new standards, laws, regulations, accounting systems, measures, etc.

Countries, cities, and other economic units can develop their own well-being-centered policy frameworks rooted in their own history and culture and try to capitalize on this to conjointly support the flourishing of human and nonhuman beings on Earth.

References

Abdallah, S., Abrar, R., & Marks, N. (2021). *The Happy Planet Index 2021 data file*. http://www.happyplanetindex.org. Accessed November 20, 2022.

Barton, D. N. (2013). *Payments for ecosystem services: Costa Rica's recipe*. https://www.eco-business.com/opinion/payments-ecosystem-services-costa-ricas-recipe/. Accessed November 20, 2022.

Bloomberg QuickTake: Originals (2018). *How Amsterdam became a bicycle paradise* [Video]. YouTube. https://www.youtube.com/watch?v=DKbRL6Opifg. Accessed November 25, 2022.

Blyth, C. A., Dalziel, R., Moran, W., Oliver, W. H., Sinclair, K., & Vowles, J. (2022). New Zealand. *Encyclopedia Britannica*. https://www.britannica.com/place/New-Zealand. Accessed November 24, 2022.

Boffey, D. (2020, April 8). Amsterdam to embrace 'doughnut' model to mend post-coronavirus economy. *The Guardian*. https://www.theguardian.com/world/2020/apr/08/amsterdam-doughnut-model-mend-post-coronavirus-economy. Accessed November 25, 2022.

Centre for Bhutan Studies & GNH Research. (2016). *A compass towards a just and harmonious society: 2015 GNH survey report*. http://www.grossnationalhappiness.com/wp-content/uploads/2017/01/Final-GNH-Report-jp-21.3.17-ilovepdf-compressed.pdf. Accessed December 1, 2022.

CoA—City of Amsterdam. (2019). *Ambitions and implementation plan 2019*. https://www.amsterdam.nl/en/policy/ambitions/. Accessed November 25, 2022.

CoA—City of Amsterdam. (2022). Policy. The Amsterdam agreement. https://www.amsterdam.nl/en/policy/. Accessed November 25, 2022.

Costanza, R. (2018). Toward a sustainable wellbeing economy. *Solutions*, *9*(2). https://thesolutionsjournal.com/toward-sustainable-wellbeing-economy/. Accessed December 10, 2025.

Costanza, R., Erickson, J. D., Farley, J., & Kubiszewski, I. (Eds.). (2020). *Sustainable wellbeing futures: A research and action agenda for ecological economics*. Edward Elgar Publishing.

Daly, H. E. (1996). *Beyond growth: The economics of sustainable development*. Beacon Press.

Daly, H. E. (2007). *Ecological economics and sustainable development*. Edward Elgar.

Davison, I. (2017, March 15). Whanganui River given legal status of a person under unique Treaty of Waitangi settlement. *New Zealand Herald*. https://www.nzherald.co.nz/whanganui-chronicle/news/whanganui-river-given-legal-status-of-a-person-under-unique-treaty-of-waitangi-settlement/JL3QKSWVZPA7XW6EN33GKU4JJ4/. Accessed on November 24, 2022.

DEAL—Doughnut Economics Action Lab. (2020). *The Amsterdam City Doughnut. A tool for transformative action*. https://doughnuteconomics.org/amsterdam-portrait.pdf. Accessed on November 25, 2022.

Dominguez, D. M. (2018). *Tourism and change in Costa Rica*. Department of Sociology, University of Oregon.

Drèze, J., & Sen, A. (2013). *An uncertain glory: India and its contradictions*. Princeton University Press.

Easterlin, R. A. (2005). Feeding the illusion of growth and happiness: A reply to hagerty and veenhoven. *Social Indicators Research*, *74*, 429–443.

Goehl, T. J. (1996). Editorial. *Environmental Health Perspectives*, *104*(6), 582–583.

GoNZ—Government of New Zealand. (2020). *The wellbeing budget 2019*. https://www.treasury.govt.nz/sites/default/files/2019-06/b19-wellbeing-budget.pdf. Accessed November 24, 2022.

GoNZ—Government of New Zealand. (2022). *Wellbeing Report. Te Tai Waiora: Wellbeing in Aotearoa New Zealand 2022*. https://www.treasury.govt.nz/publications/wellbeing-report/te-tai-waiora-2022-html#section-3. Accessed November 24, 2022.

Government of Costa Rica. (2019). *National decarbonization plan. Government of Costa Rica*. https://unfccc.int/sites/default/files/resource/NationalDecarbonizationPlan.pdf. Accessed November 20, 2022.

Happy Planet Index. (2019). https://happyplanetindex.org/wp-content/themes/hpi/public/downloads/happy-planet-index-briefing-paper.pdf. Accessed October 19, 2022.

Helmuth, C. (2000). *Culture and customs of Costa Rica*. Greenwood Press.

Honey, M. (2008). *Ecotourism and sustainable development: Who owns paradise?* Island Press.

Horton, L. (2009). Buying up nature: Economic and social impacts of Costa Rica's ecotourism boom. *Latin American Perspectives*, *36*(3), 93–107.

Human Development Index. (2022). https://hdr.undp.org/data-center/human-development-index#/indicies/HDI. Accessed October 19, 2022.

Jackson, T. (2009). *Prosperity without growth. Economics for a finite planet*. Earthscan.

Jaquiery, A. (2022, January 26). New Zealand: Changing the conversation on well-being. *IMF Country Focus*. International Monetary Fund. https://www.imf.org/en/News/Articles/2022/01/26/cf-new-zealand-changing-the-conversation-on-well-being. Accessed November 24, 2022.

Kovacs, G. (2016). A buddhista közgazdaságtan [Buddhist economics]. *Köz-Gazdaság, 11*(4), 165–175. (In Hungarian).

Kubiszewski, I., Costanza, R., Franco, C., Lawn, P., Talberth, J., Jackson, T., & Aylmer, C. (2013). Beyond GDP: Measuring and achieving global genuine progress. *Ecological Economics, 93*, 57–68.

Latouche, S. (2010). *Farewell to growth*. Polity.

Makortoff, K. (2019, January 22). Ardern: I was bood over climate views (not any more!). *The Guardian*. https://www.theguardian.com/business/live/2019/jan/22/davos-2019-financial-risks-climate-dangers-bolsonaro-attenborough-prince-william-arden-live?filterKeyEvents=false&page=with:block-5c474839e4b00173154a9368#block-5c474839e4b00173154a9368. Accessed November 24, 2022.

Max-Neef, M. (1989). *Human scale development*. Dag Hammarskjöld Foundation.

McClure, T. (2021, October 21). New Zealand becomes first country to force finance companies to act on climate risks. *The Guardian*. https://www.theguardian.com/world/2021/oct/21/new-zealand-becomes-first-country-to-force-finance-companies-to-act-on-climate-risks. Accessed November 24, 2022.

Meadows, D. H., Meadows, D. L., Randers, J., & Behrens, W. W. III. (1972). *The limits to growth: A report for the Club of Rome's project on the predicament of mankind*. Universe Books.

Miller, A. (2012). *Ecotourism development in Costa Rica: The search for oro verde*. Lexington Books.

Montmagny Grenier, C. (2020). Costa Rican beach towns as liminal spaces: Tourism, transgressions and the night-time economy. *International Journal of the Sociology of Leisure, 4*, 119–136. https://doi.org/10.1007/s41978-020-00074-z

Nugent, C. (2021, January 22). Amsterdam is embracing a radical new economic theory to help save the environment. Could it also replace capitalism? *Time*. https://time.com/5930093/amsterdam-doughnut-economics/. Accessed November 25, 2022.

Nussbaum, M. C. (2013). *Creating capabilities: The human development approach*. Belknap Press of Harvard University Press.

OECD. (2025). OECD well-being data monitor. https://www.oecd.org/en/data/tools/well-being-data-monitor/better-life-index.html. Accessed December 10, 2025.

Pagiola, S. (2008). Payments for environmental services in Costa Rica. *Ecological Economics, 65*(4), 712–724. https://doi.org/10.1016/j.ecolecon.2007.07.033

Parker, C. (2019, January 23). New Zealand will have a new 'well-being budget,' says Jacinda Ardern. *World Economic Forum*. https://www.weforum.org/agenda/2019/01/new-zealand-s-new-well-being-budget-will-fix-broken-politics-says-jacinda-ardern/. Accessed November 24, 2022.

Piketty, T. (2015). *Capital in the Twenty-first century*. Harvard University Press.

Porter, L. (2019). Looking for Pura Vida: Disgruntled parents in search of educational alternatives in Costa Rica. *Journal of Interdisciplinary Studies in Education, 8*(2), 1–20.

Raworth, K. (2017). *Doughnut economics: Seven ways to think like a twenty-first century economist*. Random House.

Rockström, J., Steffen, W., Noone, K., et al. (2009). A safe operating space for humanity. *Nature, 461*, 472–475. https://doi.org/10.1038/461472a

Saborío, A. B., Ruíz, R. L., & Davis, S. W. (2019). Practicing Pura Vida: Radiation therapy in Costa Rica. *International Journal of Radiation Oncology, Biology, Physics, 103*(4), 792–795. https://doi.org/10.1016/j.ijrobp.2018.11.022

Shrivastava, P., & Zsolnai, L. (2022). Wellbeing oriented organizations: Connecting human flourishing with ecological regeneration. *Business Ethics, the Environment & Responsibility, 31*(2), 386–397.

Skidelsky, E., & Skidelsky, R. (2012). *How much is enough? Money and the good life*. Penguin Books.

Steffen, W., et al. (2015). The trajectory of the Anthropocene: The great acceleration. *Anthropocene Review*, *2*, 81–98. https://doi.org/10.1177/2053019614564785

United Nations Climate Change. (n.d.). *Payments for environmental services program, Costa Rica*. https://unfccc.int/climate-action/momentum-for-change/financing-for-climate-friendly-investment/payments-for-environmental-services-program. Accessed November 20, 2022.

Ura, D. K. (2015). The experience of Gross National Happiness as development framework. *ADB South Asia Working Paper Series*, No. 42.

Ura, D. K., Alkire, S., & Zangmo, T. (2012). Gross National Happiness and the GNH index. Case study: Bhutan. In J. Helliwell, R. Layard, & J. Sachs (Eds.), *World happiness report–2012* (pp. 108–158). Earth Institute, Columbia University.

Valcsicsák, Z. (2015). *Álmomban Bhutánban ébredtem*. [Awakening in My Dream in Bhutan]. Oniva. (In Hungarian).

WEA—Wellbeing Economy Alliance. (2019). New Zealand announces wellbeing budget. https://weall.org/new-zealand-announces-wellbeing-budget. Accessed November 24, 2022.

WEA—Wellbeing Economy Alliance. (2022). New Zealand's first national wellbeing report. https://weall.org/new-zealands-first-national-wellbeing-report. Accessed November 24, 2022.

Weil, J. (2007). Work and anthropology in Costa Rica: An orientation. *Anthropology of Work Review*, *28*(2), 1–8.

Wellbeing Economy Alliance. (n.d.) *Costa Rica – Investing in social and ecological wellbeing*. https://weall.org/resource/costa-rica-investing-in-social-and-ecological-wellbeing. Accessed November 20, 2022.

Part IV
Holistic Methodology

Chapter 13
Identifying and Solving the Right Problems

This chapter shows that it is a serious failure of business and management practitioners when they solve the wrong problem precisely. This means that their problem formulation is inadequate, which may lead to disastrous consequences for the well-being of the stakeholders. To avoid substantive failures in problem-solving, business and management practitioners should reconsider the basic assumptions of the system under their study and include as many stakeholders' views as possible. Appropriate problem solutions should address all the important dimensions of the problem in question (the scientific-technical, the interpersonal-social, the systemic-ecological, and the existential-spiritual), and create some optimal balance among them. The job of responsible business and management is identifying the right problems and producing solutions for them that are substantively adequate and ethically acceptable in a broad socioeconomic context.

13.1 Introduction

The world is undergoing unprecedented changes and transformations in economics, business, management, technology, and politics. The responsibility of business and management is pinpointed and elevated by the current crisis, with no end in sight.

Incorrect diagnosis of the crisis and insufficient proposals for "solving" the basic problems address the responsibility of business and management practitioners who use theories and models that underline and legitimize the current flawed economic and business functioning.

This chapter is a modified version of the author's previous publication: Zsolnai, L. (2020). Identifying and Solving the Right Problem by Using Multidimensional Systems Thinking. In: Zsolnai, L., Thompson, M. (eds.) *Responsible Research for Better Business*, 35–46. Palgrave Macmillan, Cham. https://doi.org/10.1007/978-3-030-37810-3_3. Permission for reusing the paper is granted by Springer Nature.

© The Author(s), under exclusive license to Springer Nature Switzerland AG 2026

L. Zsolnai, *Planet Positive Economy*, Springer Studies in Alternative Economics,
https://doi.org/10.1007/978-3-032-21131-6_13

Highly influential but erroneous intellectual weapons of business and management include agency theory, corporate governance models, monetary incentive schemes for top management, and the shareholder value maximization model.

In ethics, the most advanced concept of responsibility was developed by German–American philosopher Hans Jonas (1984, 1996). He defines responsibility as a duty in caring for the beings affected by one's actions and policies. The beings to be considered may include human persons, social communities, nonhuman creatures, ecosystems, and future generations (Zsolnai, 2006).

Jonas underlines that moral responsibility concerns the fate of other beings. "I feel responsible, not in the first place for my conduct and its consequences but for the *matter* that has a claim on my acting." (Jonas, 1984: 92) For example, "the wellbeing, the interest, the fate of others has, by circumstance or by agreement, come to my care, which means that my control *over* it involves at the same time my obligation *for* it" (Jonas, 1984: 93).

Business and management practitioners cannot ignore the direct effects and longer-term consequences of their problem-analysis and problem-solutions on human communities, the natural environment, and future generations.

13.2 Problem Formulation

A problem is a gap between an "ought" and an "is," the difference between an ideal—something which is desired—and the actual situation as it is perceived. Important problems typically appear as "messes," which present themselves with no clear indication of how to solve them. It is neither easy to know what the ideal is, nor easy to state what the actual situation is (Ims & Zsolnai, 2009).

Mitroff and Silvers refer to John Tukey, the famous statistician, who once said: "I suspect that most failures occur because we attempt to solve the wrong problems in the first place, and not because we fail to get the right solutions to the right problems" (Mitroff & Silvers, 2009: 51). Substantive failures occur if researchers develop the solution to the wrong problem and then fool themselves into believing that they have solved the right problem to begin with.

Harvard decision theorist Howard Raiffa labeled the error of solving the wrong problem precisely as the "Error of the Third Kind." He called the error of solving the wrong problem precisely the error of the third kind because the error of the first kind and the error of the second kind were already well-known in mathematical statistics (Keeney & Raiffa, 1976).

Mitroff and Silvers (2009) notice that while the error of the first kind and the error of the second kind are taught in every course in statistics, the error of the third kind is almost never discussed. At the basic level error of the first kind and the error of the second kind involve technical knowledge. In contrast, the error of the third kind demands wisdom, the ability to exercise critical thinking (to be aware of and to challenge one's basic assumptions). Ironically, assessing the consequences of the error of the first kind and the error of the second kind involves nontechnical thinking; i.e., values and wisdom.

A revealing example of wrong problem formulation is when business and management scholars frame the main problem of managing a company as the *agency problem*. It suggests that there is an unavoidable conflict between the owners and managers of the company. Managers tend to use the resources of the company for their own material interest, which results in loss of efficiency and profit (Jensen & Meckling, 1976).

Wharton School scholar Thomas Donaldson (2012) demonstrates that this problem formulation is essentially wrong. He developed an impossibility theorem for corporate governance that clarifies how agency theory neglects normative concepts that compromise its application. For example,

> agency theory neglects to consider what general obligations, moral or otherwise, principals might have either to their agents or to other groups inside or outside the firm. (. . .) One may ask whether a manager is obliged to lie to employees (thus violating the implicit obligation to tell the truth) in order to effect a marginal benefit for shareholders, whether a manager is obliged to violate an employee's right to privacy to marginally enhance the property rights maximizing impact for shareowners, or whether a manager is obliged to engage in environmental abuse when operating in countries with insufficient environmental protections (Donaldson, 2012: 266).

For avoiding substantive errors in problem formulation, different advices have been developed. Russell Ackoff (2004) suggested reconsidering the basic assumptions of the system under question. Ian Mitroff (1998) urges to include as many stakeholders' views as possible in the process of problem formulation.

Business and management practitioners need to employ *holistic thinking* to define the right problem. Assumptions about the stakeholders and their broader social context should be scrutinized. Business and management research should define the right stakeholders, and this generally means expanding the set of conventionally accepted stakeholders. Defining the right problem precisely is indispensable for avoiding the error of the third kind.

The systems methodology developed by Ackoff (2004) at the Wharton School of University of Pennsylvania states that a system's performance is determined by the adequacy of the basic assumptions on which it functions and on the way the system is capable of pursuing its objectives. Problems indicate that basic assumptions are inadequate and/or the system is incapable of performing adequately.

Corporate governance models typically favor institutional arrangements in which executives are accountable to the Board of Directors and not directly to the shareholders or other representatives of society. This kind of arrangement makes it easy for corporate executives to avoid full responsibility for their decisions and policies affecting the future of the company and the well-being of diverse stakeholders, including the company's stockholders. In this way, corporate executives are discouraged from serving as guardians of society's vital interests. The result is corporate "short-termism" and malfunctions even from a narrow economic point of view.

13.3 Developing Substantively Adequate and Ethically Acceptable Solutions

Solutions developed for business and management problems are never ethically neutral. They confirm or violate ethical claims of the stakeholders and generate different payoffs for them. The use of multidimensional systems thinking may help practitioners to generate solutions for business and management problems that are substantively adequate and ethically acceptable in a broad socioeconomic context.

The standard solution to the agency problem is to provide managers of the company with high monetary incentives, including excessive pay and bonuses. This solution may become counterproductive as it usually generates adverse effects on managerial performance and creates negative effects for the employees and society at large.

High monetary incentives may have an adverse effect on managerial performance in a broad sense. Ims et al. (2014) argue that one-dimensional economic incentives may crowd out existential, social, and ecological values that influence the manager's commitment to ensure responsible business conduct, and have negative spillover effects that reduce the manager's performance (Bouckaert, 2006; Ims & Zsolnai, 2009; Mitroff, 1998).

Ims et al. (2014) show how high-level compensation crowds out not only the intrinsic motivation of managers, but also existential, social, and ecological value considerations that influence managers' commitment to responsible business conduct. Excessive compensation schemes may be detrimental to the inclinations of managers and their organizations to act responsibly. The crowding-out effect is often referred to as "the hidden cost of reward" (Deci, 1976). It can be called the hidden existential, social, and ecological costs of the one-dimensionality of business and management conduct. This is an instructive example of a highly complex problem with a single-dimensional solution. It shows that a wrong problem framework may lead to solutions that are not only wrong but may be harmful.

Mitroff (1998) suggests that there are four basic, irreducible dimensions of any important problem: the technical-scientific, the interpersonal-social, the systemic-ecological, and the existential-spiritual (Fig. 13.1). Practitioners should use all these dimensions as an integrated framework for problem identification to avoid solving the wrong problem.

The *technical-scientific* dimension is the dominant perspective in today's business and management thinking and favors technical solutions to problems, even when other solutions are more appropriate. This techno-centric bias is partly explained by the status and prestige that engineers and economists enjoy in our culture. This dimension also dominates today's business and management research by focusing on scientific rigor without corresponding attention to the relevance of the topic for use in the real world.

The *interpersonal-social* dimension concerns the way the problem is perceived from a social, group, and family point of view. Social relationships and social

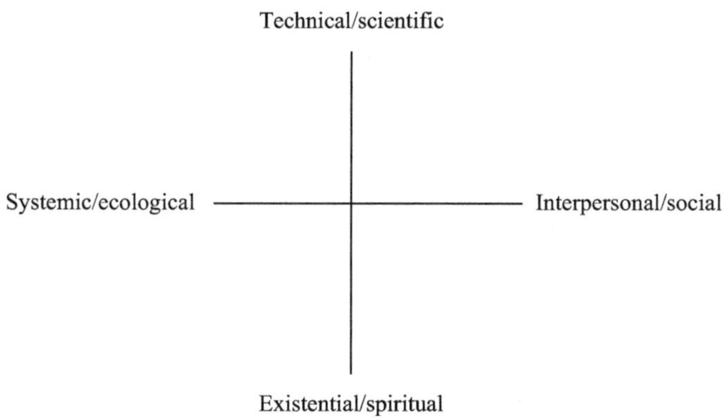

Fig. 13.1 The four quadrants model of Ian Mitroff. *Source* Author' own creation

issues get a lot less attention than production efficiency and performance outcomes in the mainstream research agenda (Walsh et al., 2003).

The *systemic-ecological* dimension takes into consideration the long-term consequences of how the problem is solved. It assumes that all things are interconnected. This dimension involves the perspectives of future generations and nature and goes beyond geographic borders and narrow time limits. The finance and business management literature almost completely lacks the discussion of the vital connections between economic functioning and Earth systems processes and hence disregards most of the negative effects of business and management practices on nature and future generations (Shrivastava et al., 2019).

The *existential-spiritual* dimension emphasizes the lives and fates of individual human beings and the impacts on their life-worlds. Feelings and meaning are important aspects in this dimension. The important existential questions are as follows: Who am I? Who do I want to be? How do my actions influence my life project? What gives meaning and purpose to my life? Ultimately, all important decisions and acts influence the self of the decision makers and decision receivers. It is important to emphasize the existential-spiritual dimension because it is usually ignored or even denied in mainstream social science literature (Zsolnai & Flanagan, 2019). It is almost nonexisting in business and management research too. Yet we cannot ignore that organizations are social systems with people who have deeply held feelings and spirits (Ims & Zsolnai, 2009).

Finding appropriate solutions for business and management problems requires addressing all dimensions of the problem (the technical-scientific, the interpersonal-social, the systemic-ecological, and the existential-spiritual) and integrating them into solutions that create a new balance among them. Ethics is implicated by any problem solution, so it is worthwhile to evaluate more explicitly the generated problem solutions through the lens of ethics.

Ethics offers two main paradigms that are the most relevant for assessing the ethical validity of solutions developed for business and management problems

(Verschuren & Zsolnai, 1998). One such paradigm is called "consequentialism," while the other is called "deontology." Consequentialism bases the evaluation of a problem solution solely on its real-world consequences. In this paradigm, ethical value depends on the goodness of consequences for the stakeholders. Contrary to this, deontology favors the evaluation of a problem solution on the basis of its correspondence to the relevant ethical norms. In this paradigm, ethical value depends on ethical rightness, which corresponds to the norms. Deontology disregards the actual consequences of a problem solution.

Verschuren and Zsolnai (1998) argue that one has to use *both* the consequentialist and the deontological paradigms in assessing the ethical value of solutions developed for business and management problems. Multidimensional systems thinking also applies here. Solving the right problem should consider both ethical principles. A holistic approach would be explicit about these two considerations and avoid compromising one principle with the exclusive focus on the other principle.

The external value of a problem solution is largely determined by its service to the stakeholders. A solution can be considered good if it meets the needs and wants of the stakeholders. The limitations of this approach can be surpassed if one introduces deontological considerations into the evaluation. Certainly, a solution should satisfy the basic ethical norms that are commonly accepted by the community of stakeholders and the general public. How well a solution comes up to the relevant ethical norms constitutes the intrinsic value of the solution.

Excessive pay for business executives has been criticized by many stakeholder groups as well as the general public. Many people, including politicians and employees, believe that the extremely high salaries and bonuses of business executives violate the principles of fairness and social justice (Frey & Osterloh, 2005). Also, monetary incentives induce corporate behavior that results in detrimental effects, which may lead to further destruction of the company and its business ecosystem (Ims et al., 2014).

13.4 Conclusion

A distinctive characteristic of responsible business and management is that it aims to solve the right problems in substantively adequate and ethically acceptable ways in a broad socioeconomic context. This involves defining the problems in the right form and developing solutions that meet the relevant ethical norms of the stakeholders and generate true benefits for them.

To avoid substantive failures in problem formulation, business and management practitioners should reconsider the basic underlying assumptions of the system they study and should investigate the chosen problem from a wide range of perspectives, taking the views of different stakeholders into consideration.

To avoid failures in developing solutions, business and management practitioners may use multidimensional systems methodologies. Appropriate solutions address all the important dimensions of the problem in question (the technical-scientific, the interpersonal-social, the systemic-ecological, and the existential-spiritual), and create some optimal balance among them. Business and management practitioners are advised to evaluate their solutions from a deontological point of view (Which ethical norms are violated or satisfied?) and also from a consequentialist point of view (What are the payoffs for different stakeholders?).

References

Ackoff, R. (2004). *Ackoff center guiding principles*. The Wharton School, University of Pennsylvania.
Bouckaert, L. (2006). The ethics management paradox. In L. Zsolnai (Ed.), *Interdisciplinary yearbook of business ethics* (pp. 191–194). Peter Lang.
Deci, E. L. (1976). The hidden cost of rewards. *Organizational Dynamics*, *4*(3), 61–72.
Donaldson, T. (2012). The epistemic fault line in corporate governance. *Academy of Management Review*, *37*(2), 256–271.
Frey, B., & Osterloh, M. (2005). Yes, managers should be paid like bureaucrats. *Journal of Management Inquiry*, *14*(1), 96–111.
Ims, K. J., Pedersen, L. J., & Zsolnai, L. (2014). How economic incentives destroy social, ecological and existential values: The case of executive compensation. *Journal of Business Ethics*, *123*(2), 353–360.
Ims, K. J., & Zsolnai, L. (2009). Holistic problem solving. In L. Zsolnai & A. Tencati (Eds.), *The future international manager: A vision of the roles and duties of management* (pp. 116–129). Palgrave-Macmillan.
Jensen, M. C., & Meckling, W. H. (1976). Theory of the firm: Managerial behavior, agency costs and ownership structure. *Journal of Financial Economics*, *3*(4), 305–360.
Jonas, H. (1984). *The imperative of responsibility: In search of an ethics for the technological age*. The University of Chicago Press.
Jonas, H. (1996). *Mortality and morality. A search for the good after Auschwitz*. Northwestern University Press.
Keeney, R. L., & Raiffa, H. (1976). *Decisions with multiple objectives: Preferences and value tradeoffs*. Wiley.
Mitroff, I. (1998). *Smart thinking for crazy times: The art of solving the right problems*. Berrett-Koehler Publishers, Inc.
Mitroff, I., & Silvers, A. (2009). *Dirty rotten strategies—How we trick ourselves and others into solving the wrong problems precisely*. Stanford University Press.
Shrivastava, P., Zsolnai, L., Wasieleski, D., Stafford-Smith, M., Walker, T., Weber, O., Krosinsky, C., & Oram, D. (2019). Finance and management for the Anthropocene. *Organization & Environment*, *32*(1), 26–40.
Verschuren, P., & Zsolnai, L. (1998). Norms, goals and stakeholders in program evaluation. *Human Systems Management*, *17*(2), 155–160.
Walsh, J. P., Weber, K., & Margolis, J. D. (2003). Social issues and management: Our lost cause found. *Journal of Management*, *29*(6), 859–881.
Zsolnai, L. (2006). Extended stakeholder theory. *Society and Business Review*, *1*(1), 37–44.
Zsolnai, L., & Flanagan, B. (Eds.). (2019). *The Routledge international handbook of spirituality in society and the professions*. Routledge.

Chapter 14
Methodology for Systems Change

This chapter presents different levels of intervention in a system (parameters, feedback, design, and purpose). Then it classifies strategies for interacting with organizations ("non-cooperation," "reforming," "cooperation," and "creating") to help avoid social and environmental ills or produce socioecological well-being.

14.1 Leverage Points of Systems Change

There are many options for changing systems, ranging from small (yet possibly important) tweaks to the wholesale re-envisioning of what systems are for. Based on the "systems thinking" approach (Meadows, 1999; Abson et al., 2017), it is possible to identify different leverage points in complex systems, from parameters through feedback and design to underlying intent (Shrivastava et al., 2019) (See Table 14.1).

Considering the levels of intervention in a system, we can suggest modifications in the stakeholder management practice of economic players. Accordingly, (i) the definition of stakeholder should be revised to emphasize ecological prominence, thereby supporting the well-being of present and future generations. (ii) The principles of stakeholder management should be expanded to include sustainability values across all stakeholders. (iii) The underlying institutional logics should be reframed so that economic players envision their goals and purpose in relation to their long-term value creation for human and nonhuman entities. (iv) Evaluations of the quality of stakeholder relationships should be restructured so that sustainability is part of the function of every stakeholder interaction with an economic actor (Shrivastava et al., 2019: 36).

© The Author(s), under exclusive license to Springer Nature Switzerland AG 2026

L. Zsolnai, *Planet Positive Economy*, Springer Studies in Alternative Economics,
https://doi.org/10.1007/978-3-032-21131-6_14

Table 14.1 Levels of interventions in a system

System characteristic	Description	Meadows' leverage points
Parameters	Relatively mechanistic characteristics	Parameters, the magnitude of buffers compared to the structure of material stocks and flows
Feedbacks	Interactions between elements within a system that drive internal dynamics	Length of feedback delays compared to rates of system change, strength of negative feedback, and gains associated with positive feedback loops
Design	Social structures and institutions that manage feedback and parameters	Access to information flows, rules of the system (incentives, constraints), power to change/self-organize system structure
Purpose	Underpinning values, goals, and worldviews of actors that shape the emergent direction to which the system is oriented	Goals of the system, mindset/paradigm from which the system arises, and the power to transcend paradigms

Source Adapted from Shrivastava et al. (2019, p. 31)

14.2 Strategies for Interacting with Organizations

For economic players, different strategies are available for managing the problems of living and functioning in a world dominated by institutions occupied with materialistic values.

We can differentiate among "non-cooperation," "reforming," "cooperation," and "creating" strategies, which can be applied selectively when one interacts with different types of organizations (Zsolnai, 2022). In this way, the following options emerge. (i) Noncooperation with destructive, unethical organizations. Related activities include boycotting their products and services, divesting resources from them, minimizing collaboration with them, and fighting against their functioning. (ii) Reforming destructive, unethical organizations. This includes reducing or mitigating the negative impacts of their functioning, modifying their criteria for success, improving their working models, and changing their mindsets. (iii) Cooperation with progressive, ethical organizations. This includes popularizing their functioning, maximizing collaboration with them, investing resources in them, and using their products and services. And (iv) creating progressive, ethical organizations. This includes initiating progressive visions for them, gathering people and resources, developing new working models, and implementing and continuously improving their functioning (Zsolnai, 2022).

Transitioning toward a planet-positive economy may require using all of these strategies in different situations in different ways.

References

Abson, D. J., Fischer, J., Leventon, J., Newig, J., Schomerus, T., Vilsmaier, U., & Jager, N. W. (2017). Leverage points for sustainability transformation. *AMBIO: A Journal of the Human Environment, 46*(1), 30–39.

Meadows, D. (1999). *Leverage points: Places to intervene in a system*. Sustainability Institute.

Shrivastava, P., Zsolnai, L., Wasieleski, D., Stafford-Smith, M., Walker, T., Weber, O., Krosinsky, C., & Oram, D. (2019). Finance and management for the Anthropocene. *Organization & Environment, 32*(1), 26–40.

Zsolnai, L. (2022). The awakened brain. The psychology of spirituality and our search for meaning by Lisa Miller. *Journal of Management, Spirituality & Religion, 19*(5), 546–549.

Part V
Ethics in Dark Times

Chapter 15
Ethics Needs Spirituality

This chapter discusses the relationship between ethics and spirituality. It shows that business ethics lacks a deeper existential-spiritual foundation, leading to the inadequate and ineffective functioning of ethics in business and management. The chapter argues for spirituality-based ethics in business and management.

15.1 Ethics Is Devoid of Spirituality

Mainstream paradigms of ethics, including business ethics, are devoid of references to spirituality or religion. They employ a materialistic and individualistic conception of human nature in which humans are viewed as materialistic beings with only materialistic desires and motivations. Contemporary ethics suggests that ethical action is a cognitive enterprise. Today's dominant ethical theories provide abstract models to be applied by moral agents. But the main problem of ethical behavior is not ethical knowledge but ethical *motivation*, as recent findings from moral psychology show (Bandura, 2015).

As mentioned earlier in this book, world-renowned psychologist Bandura (2015) has identified eight psychosocial mechanisms by which considerate moral agents can engage in harmful and socially injurious conduct. These moral disengagement mechanisms include moral justification, euphemistic labeling, advantageous comparison, displacement of responsibility, diffusion of responsibility, disregarding or distorting consequences, dehumanization, and the attribution of blame.

The functioning of moral disengagement mechanisms makes ethics ineffective or even counterproductive in many cases, including in major industries such as the gun, entertainment, tobacco, and financial industries (Bandura, 2015).

Spirituality makes people less likely to employ moral disengagement mechanisms (Baron et al., 2015) and provides them with greater opportunities for effective moral functioning. Empirical evidence suggests that spiritual experiences help people

© The Author(s), under exclusive license to Springer Nature Switzerland AG 2026
L. Zsolnai, *Planet Positive Economy*, Springer Studies in Alternative Economics,
https://doi.org/10.1007/978-3-032-21131-6_15

transcend their narrow self-conceptions, exercise genuine empathy with others, and adopt an all-encompassing perspective. Spiritual experiences involve authentic experimental identification with other people, animals, plants, and various other aspects of nature and the cosmos (Grof, 1998).

15.2 The Ethics Management Paradox

Reducing ethics to a functional, instrumental management tool may crowd out genuine moral feelings and moral commitment, leading to less ethical functioning. We must be aware of the paradox of ethical management when substituting ethics for technocratic management approaches.

The core idea of the *Ethics Management Paradox* can be stated as follows (Bouckaert, 2006, Bouckaert & Zsolnai 2011). By creating new regulations to temper opportunistic behavior in and among organizations, we often reinforce the underlying roots of opportunism. We may introduce economic incentive-like benefits, such as premiums or tax relief, for those who respect the new regulations, but by doing this, we substitute moral feelings for economic calculations. Hence, the paradox emerges: the more ethical management, the less ethics *in* management. Preaching moral concepts such as trust, responsibility, or democracy grounded on calculative self-interest or as conditions of systemic functionality is ambiguous. It opens the door to suspicion and distrust because calculations and systemic conditions can easily be manipulated. "When the fox preaches, guard your geese."

It is fascinating to see how trust, value-driven leadership and democratic stakeholding have become part of Western management theory. But we must be aware of their paradoxical characteristics. The more economic democracy can be sustained by rational and economic discourse, the more it risks crowding out moral commitment, which is a necessary condition for sustaining genuine entrepreneurship and stakeholding. Thus, we must raise not only the question of how to operationalize business ethics, but also how to make it genuinely ethical.

The ethics management paradox refers to the gap between expectations regarding whether ethics management improves the ethicality of business and the reality that this is not always the case. In 2008, a bubble burst and brought us the banking crisis, followed by an economic recession. The surprising fact is that before the crisis, many of the companies and banks that were involved had invested in programs of corporate social responsibility and business ethics. But these efforts failed because ethics management was reduced to a business management tool.

The ethics management paradox implies a search for spirituality as a way to transcend the instrumental rationality that creates the paradox. Spirituality—defined as an inner experience of deep interconnectedness with all living beings—opens up distance from the pressures of the market and the routines of business as usual. This distance seems to be a necessary condition for developing innovative ethical ideas and practices. It may restore intrinsic motivation and provide a long-term horizon. Unfortunately, spirituality is not yet a mainstream concept in the business world.

In business, instrumental and utilitarian rationality is still the dominant perspective, whereas spirituality is anchored in the deeper, noninstrumental, and nonutilitarian experience of life. Business can be renewed and transformed into a progressive social institution if it enriches itself by taking spirituality seriously and putting it at the core of its activities (Bouckaert & Zsolnai 2011).

Ethical codes and professional ethics formulate rights and duties for all relevant stakeholders to avoid a clash of interests. However, there is a zone of wicked problems that remain unsolvable and difficult to overcome. By divergent problems, Schumacher refers to problems which are linked with antagonistic and unconciliatory value premises. Ethical codes, which mainly protect the interests and power of the regulating authorities, do not solve these kinds of problems. At best, they help us to keep value conflicts under control. We need other ways to overcome deeply rooted conflicts of values.

Spirituality as a discipline has the potential to disclose meaning and purpose in life that overcomes the drive for self-interest, polarization, and conflicts of values. We can consider spirituality as intuitive, nonrational thinking that opens our mind to the co-creation of meaning in life. Spiritual methods include practicing empathy, dialogical thinking, storytelling, symbolic visualizations, meditation, self-reflection, prayer, etc. Spirituality helps to move beyond blocks and may reveal new perspectives that enable us to transcend them and to find new ways of being and acting.

The interlinked ecological, social, and economic crises clearly show the inadequacy of the materialistic management paradigm. Materialistic management is based on the belief that the primary motivation for doing business is money-making and that success should be measured by profit only (Zsolnai, 2015). A postmaterialistic management paradigm is emerging that is characterized by frugality, deep ecology, trust, reciprocity, responsibility for future generations, and authenticity. Within this framework, profit and growth are no longer ultimate aims but elements of a wider set of goals. Similarly, cost-benefit calculations are no longer the essence of management but part of a broader concept of wisdom in leadership.

References

Bandura, A. (2015). *Moral disengagement: How good people can do harm and feel good about themselves*. Palgrave-Macmillan.

Baron, R. A., Zhao, H., & Miao, Q. (2015). Personal motives, moral disengagement, and unethical decisions by entrepreneurs: Cognitive mechanisms on the 'slippery slope'. *Journal of Business Ethics*, *128*, 107–118.

Bouckaert, L. (2006). The ethics management paradox. In L. Zsolnai (Ed.), *Interdisciplinary yearbook of business ethics* (pp. 191–194). Peter Lang Academic Publishers.

Bouckaert, L., & Zsolnai, L. (Eds.). (2011). *The Palgrave handbook of spirituality and business*. Palgrave-Macmillan.

Grof, S. (1998). *The cosmic game: Explorations of the frontiers of human consciousness*. State University of New York Press.

Zsolnai, L. (2015). *Post-materialistic business: Spiritual value-orientation in renewing management*. Palgrave.

Chapter 16
Care, and Its Relevance to Today's Economy

Care is a central aspect of human existence. What we care about and whom we care for largely determine our way of being. The subjects of care present a frame of reference for our human functioning.

The survival of the fittest and other Darwinian notions have become slogans for the business world, which favors competitive, instrumental, and capitalist values. However, in his *The Descent of Man,* Charles Darwin wrote the following:

> Important as the struggle for existence has been and even still is, yet as far as the highest part of our nature is concerned there are other agencies more important. For the moral qualities are advanced either directly or indirectly much more through the efforts of habit, by our reasoning powers, by instruction, by religion, etc., than through natural selection (Darwin, 1871: 403-404).

Loye (2009) found that in "The Descent of Man" Darwin wrote 95 times about love, 92 times about moral sensitivity, 12 times about competition, and 27 times about cooperation, called mutual aid in Darwin's time. Loye added furthermore that for Darwin, the prime driver for human evolution—and completion of his theory of evolution was our capacity for the "moral sense," i.e., moral sensitivity, an evolutionary inbuilt thrust within us for the development of a sense of right versus wrong.

Care and ethics, then, are considered by Darwin as higher-level imperatives, and more important than fighting and competition.

Care is essential to our life, and caring is an essential part of who we are.

We need care for our survival. Attachment theory (Bowlby, 1982) proposes that all individuals are born with an innate desire to seek proximity to others in times of

---

This chapter is a modified version of the previously published paper by Ora Setter and the author: Setter, O., Zsolnai, L. (2019). Care, and Its Relevance to Today's Economy. In: Setter, O., Zsolnai, L. (eds.) *Caring Management in the New Economy*, 3–20. Palgrave Macmillan, Cham. https://doi.org/10.1007/978-3-030-14199-8_1. Permission for reusing the paper is granted by Springer Nature.

© The Author(s), under exclusive license to Springer Nature Switzerland AG 2026
L. Zsolnai, *Planet Positive Economy*, Springer Studies in Alternative Economics,
https://doi.org/10.1007/978-3-032-21131-6_16

need or distress in order to enhance their survival prospects. Children, as well as other mammalian infants, are largely unable to feed or protect themselves, as their survival is dependent on their ability to maintain proximity to older, wiser, and more capable adults. The ability of an individual to form an emotional and physical "attachment" to another person—by being taken care of—gives them a sense of stability and the security necessary to take risks, branch out, and grow and develop as a personality. This sense of security (or lack there of) then becomes the basis of their own individual style of attachment, which then remains relatively fixed over the lifespan of the individual. Ainsworth et al. (2015) discovered that attachment formation is an "innate" or instinctive form of human behavior.

Caring for others is also an essential part of our humanity. Our brain is wired to react empathetically to the pain of others as a means of signaling danger and eliciting help. Functional MRI scans show that if an individual watches someone undergo electric shock, their brain lights up in the same areas as those in the brain of the person in pain (Bufalari et al., 2007). When we have feelings of caring or love for other people, we feel better. Moreover, a growing body of evidence shows that providing care can be beneficial to the caregiver, leading to reduced stress, increased happiness, and an increased sense of social connectedness (Inagaki & Orehek, 2017).

16.1 Care in Organizations, Caring Organizations

Within organizational settings, caring is usually thought of as pertaining either to leadership roles or to team and peer social ties. But from the organizational or management point of view, there are more stakeholders to care about.

The problem of care appears in management in relation to how to manage the stakeholders of an organization. Stakeholder theory (Freeman et al., 2010) says that businesses and other organizations should consider the interests and claims of stakeholders and manage their activities accordingly. From this perspective, the effective management of stakeholders is a strategic activity that is necessary for the success and long-term survival of an organization. Ignoring stakeholders is dangerous, not just because it is morally inappropriate, but also because it does not make economic sense.

There are two interrelated problems with the stakeholder approach: (i) the narrow conception of stakeholders, and (ii) the fallibility of stakeholders concerning their own well-being (Zsolnai, 2018).

Companies usually narrowly define their stakeholders. Only owners, managers, employees, creditors, suppliers, and local communities are considered stakeholders. This narrow definition of stakeholders is often a recipe for disaster in terms of organizational functioning. Mitroff (1998) argues that when stakeholders are defined too narrowly, and/or are not identified correctly, this leads to solving the wrong problems precisely. When managers confront a problem that is located at the edge of their competence, especially a novel problem, or a case outside the bounds of accepted thinking and practice, they are either stymied to the point of paralysis, or fall back on the only resource they have: reducing a novel or unique situation to a problem that they already know how to solve. “The trouble is that the problems that one knows how to solve may bear little resemblance to the actual problems one needs to solve. As a result, extreme cases and outlier problems and situations pose a real and a serious challenge to the professions and to accepted modes of thinking. In the extreme, they lead to serious errors, catastrophic failures, and major disasters and crises” (Mitroff & Silvers, 2009).

Psychology and behavioral economics have revealed that people are rather poor at predicting their own future well-being. They are fallible in understanding what they will like in the future, and how they will feel in future states of affairs. Based on experimental research, Nobel Prize-winning Kahneman (2011) states that people are myopic in their decisions, lack skills at predicting their future tastes, and can be led to make erroneous choices through their fallible memories and incorrect evaluations of past experiences.

Kahneman (2011) suggests differentiating between experienced utility and predicted utility. The experienced utility of an outcome is a measure of the hedonic experience of that outcome. The predicted utility of an outcome is defined as the individual’s beliefs about its experienced utility at some future time. Predicted utility is an ex-ante variable, while experienced utility is an ex-post variable in the decision-making process.

According to the rational choice model used in stakeholder theory, decisions are made based on predicted utility. If experienced utility greatly differs from predicted utility, then this may lead to subrational, or even irrational, choices. The problem of predicted utility raises the question, “Do people actually know what they will like?” The answer is a definite “No.” The accuracy of people’s hedonic predictions is generally quite poor (Kahneman, 2011).

Related experimental studies suggest two conclusions: (i) people may have little ability to forecast changes in their hedonic responses to stimuli; and (ii) even in situations that permit accurate hedonic predictions, people may tend to make decisions about future consumption without due consideration of possible changes in their tastes (Kahneman, 2011).

Since people use their evaluative memories to guide their choices about future outcomes, deceptive retrospective evaluations may lead to erroneous choices. Kahneman (2011) identifies two major obstacles to maximizing experienced utility. (i) People lack skill at predicting how their tastes might change; thus, it is difficult to describe as rational agents those individuals who are prone to making large errors when predicting what they will want or enjoy in the future. The other obstacle is a tendency of individuals to use the affect associated with particular moments as a proxy for the utility of extended outcomes. Errors in lessons drawn from experience will inevitably be reflected in deficient choices about the future (Kahneman, 2011).

Managing for a narrowly defined set of stakeholders cannot guarantee that the functioning of an organization is ecologically sustainable or beneficial for society more generally, including future generations. Considering the interests of stakeholders solely based on the latter's own calculations may lead to unacceptable outcomes. Businesses and other organizations should expand their set of stakeholders and go beyond trying to meet goals rationally founded on calculated self-interest.

In his opus magnum, *The Imperative of Responsibility: In Search of an Ethics for the Technological Age*, Jonas (1984) describes the impact of modern technology on the human condition as follows:

1. The nature of human activities has been altered and enlarged due to their magnitude and novelty, and their impact on man's global future.
2. Responsibility is correlated to power, and must be commensurate with the latter's scope and its exercise.
3. To replace the former projections of hope, an imaginative 'heuristics of fear' should be developed to inform us of what may be at stake, and what we must beware of.
4. Ethics are created and underpinned by how man perceives his duties towards himself, his distant posterity, and the plenitude of life under his dominion (Jonas, 1984: x).

Jonas (1984) argues that an imperative of responsibility might be framed like this: "Act so that the effects of your action are compatible with the permanence of genuine human life" (Jonas, 1984: 11). Or, expressed negatively: "Act so that the effects of your action are not destructive of the future possibility of such life" (Jonas, 1984: 11).

Human responsibility is never formal, but it is always substantive. It involves humans being responsible not primarily for their own conduct and its consequences, but for the matter that has or will make a claim on present action. The well-being, the interests, the fates of others have, by circumstance or by agreement, come into *our care*, which means that our control over them involves at the same time our obligation towards them (Jonas, 1984).

The imperative of responsibility implies that nature, human beings, and future generations should be accepted as primary subjects of care in business (Zsolnai, 2018). Business actors must develop practices that incorporate genuine interest in and caring for the existence and well-being of these primordial "stakeholders." The following issues and themes illustrate some of the different ways (and practical models of how) this may be possible.

16.2 Issues and Themes of Care and Caring

In his paper, "Authentic Human Relations and the Economy," Ungvari-Zrinyi (2019) reflects on the ideas of Martin Buber in terms of establishing authentic human, social, and environmental relations in today's economy, which is characterized by pervasive problems such as growing inequality, alienation from the workplace, precarious work, work-life imbalance, consumerism, and environmental decay.

Ungvari-Zrinyi (2019) suggests that Buber's (1937) philosophy of dialogue is a good starting point for re-conceptualizing current economic and social thought. In Buber's philosophy, the clear distinction between personal, authentic relationships ("I-Thou") and objectifying relations ("I–It") is central. In an I–Thou relation, one person confirms the other as being of unique value, and a sense of mutual responsibility is created, whereas people engaged in the objectifying relation of I–It tend to reduce relationships to their use value.

The distinction between authentic and inauthentic human relations is a good basis for the criticism of the idea of *Homo Economicus*—which is an artificial device in economic theorizing whose essence is far from that of a real human being who is faced with complex challenges and takes responsibility for others. Ungvari-Zrinyi (2019) shows that Buber's philosophy of human encounters can be used to address the contemporary problems of economy and society, including encounters with people of different faiths, different nationalities, and even nonhuman beings.

Rifkin's (2010) idea of the "empathic civilization" appears to be relevant here. Rifkin considers empathy to be the ability of human beings to show solidarity—not only to each other, but also towards their fellow non-human creatures with whom they share the planet. In agreement with Rifkin, Ungvari-Zrinyi (2019) believes that new technologies are allowing people to connect their empathy "to the entire human race in a single biosphere." People are not just "materialistic, self-interested, utilitarian, pleasure-seeking" creatures, but beings at various stages of consciousness, and theological, ideological, and psychological development. The emergence of an empathic civilization seems to be a consequence of the existential similarity of finite beings, combined with the possibilities engendered by the third industrial revolution. Ungvari–Zrinyi emphasizes that we find this vision in the religious (Chassidic) spirituality of Buber's philosophy.

In his paper, "Caring for Being and Caring for Other," Bouckaert (2019) argues that caring can be considered to be an attitude that underlies all human activities. Bouckaert recalls that in his "Sein und Zeit," German philosopher Heidegger (1927) developed an ontological analysis of care (*Sorge*) as the basic structure of our being-in-the-world (*Dasein*). Confronted with the threat of death, human beings are driven by anxiety and worry. Hence, their first act of caring concerns their survival and the meaning of their own threatened existence. But Bouckaert (2019) warns that, in sharp contrast with Heidegger's concept of care, French Jewish philosopher Levinas (1961) interprets caring as a nonchosen responsibility for the other. Bouckaert (2019) believes that caring for the other is a more genuine starting point than having concern about one's own existence.

Bouckaert (2019) explores the notion of "vulnerability" and differentiates between negative and positive forms of it. The Heidegger–Levinas controversy comes to the fore when one addresses the question of which and whose vulnerability should be awarded priority. Bouckaert applies caring to the sphere of economics and highlights the contrast between philanthropy and relational economics as two different forms of economic care. He illustrates the implications of the Heidegger–Levinas dilemma with a business case taken from Goethe's *Faust*. As a successful entrepreneur, Faust is confronted with a choice between entrepreneurial success and caring for others. In the early nineteenth century, Goethe was optimistic about economic progress, but today we need a much stronger focus on addressing the vulnerability of our planet and of people.

Bouckaert (2019) suggests that our notion of progress must *not* be primarily embedded in a notion of mastering the world. We need a type of caring entrepreneurship inspired by a deep understanding of our human condition and the vulnerability of our planet. This can be supported by concrete practices of relational economics, servant leadership, and sustainability. To avoid escapism, future managers need to have concrete confrontations with the most vulnerable forms of life upon our planet, which deserve a better future.

In his paper, "Getting to the Heart of Compassion in Philosophy and Economic Life," Jackson (2019) links philosophical reflection with business-and-society considerations concerning a culture of compassion for economic life. He explores the concept of compassion, revealing it as a primordial feature of the human condition. Jackson highlights several of the tensions that attend alternative interpretations of the concept of compassion that appear throughout ancient, medieval, modern, and postmodern treatments in the Western philosophical tradition. He then proceeds to extend some of these interpretative perspectives about compassion into contemporary economic life, focusing on models of hybrid social enterprise.

Jackson (2019) uses the examples of Yunus' (2011) social enterprise and Porter and Kramer's (2011) shared value model as illustrations, but many other socially-engaged business models and initiatives within the "conscious capitalism" movement may be classified into the same category (benefit-corporations, certified B-corps, economy of communion, cross-compensation, and market-connection frameworks). Jackson (2019) emphasizes that supporting both Yunus' social enterprising and Porter and Kramer's shared value model is the notion that the logic of gift and the logic of exchange exist in a state of tension that involves counterbalancing opposing elements, such as the promptings of love with the restraints of justice. In facing that challenge, Jackson believes compassion can constitute a motivation and inspiration for prosocial entrepreneurial business solutions in our deeply divided and profoundly needy world.

In his paper, "Consciousness Approach to Management and Economics," Jacobs (2019) recalls the importance of *consciousness* in business and management. He refers to Steve Jobs of Apple as an embodiment of the spiritual principle that one person can change the world. This case also illustrates the spiritual power behind the aspiration of the human spirit for freedom, empowerment, and mastery, rather than passive submission to the machinery of technology and mechanisms of social organization. Jobs perceived the powerful stirrings of a deep evolutionary social movement, and Apple delivered creative, new products to meet this. Apple's collective accomplishments, like those of Leonardo da Vinci and the Italian Renaissance, exemplify the virtually infinite potential for innovation and creativity.

Jacobs (2019) emphasizes the value of values. Values determine the ultimate level of accomplishment. Values are an expression of what we regard as valuable. The power of values depends on the intensity and sincerity with which we value them. Values embrace all aspects of life and encompass the subjective as well as the objective dimension. But, aside from their specific individual relevance, they always reflect on and refer back to a whole that is greater than the sum of its parts, for the implementation of any value necessarily requires the implementation of many others. The perfect manifestation of any value requires a perfect manifestation of the whole, which is one.

Jacobs (2019) states that a spiritual view of life and management involves responsibility and relationships as inseparably interdependent factors—for the latter is based on the premise that the outer objective conditions in which we live and act and the inner subjective conditions that constitute our personal consciousness are intimately related. The outer world influences and, in most circumstances, shapes, defines, directs, and limits our consciousness. The essence of spirituality is to discover that reality within ourselves is not determined by the external social and physical conditions around us, but is free and untouched by its pressures and compulsions. It also tells us that, once free, we discover that we have the capacity to alter the conditions around us not only through the action which we initiate, but also, and much more powerfully, by acting on and altering our own consciousness. When we do that, we discover the deeper truth that the inner always determines the outer; our inner consciousness always determines our response to the conditions of external work on us. In this way, consciousness means the power to change things in our lives, including management and business.

In his paper, "New Metrics for a New Economy," Kahane (2019) states that there is an urgent need for a paradigm shift towards a new multidimensional, multiobjective economy that serves a diversity of values alongside economic goals. In such an economy, "doing good" (socially, environmentally, and ethically) will support rather than stand in contradiction to "doing well" (economically). The level of environmental and social threats is developing at an exponential rate, and the need for drastic transformation is pressing.

Kahane (2019) warns that any system is guided by the metrics it uses. Metrics do not merely serve as tools for measuring results. They actually act as a compass or dashboard, leading us on our way. Using inappropriate metrics leads us in the wrong direction. At present, we serve the economy, rather than having the economy serve our values. In recent years, there have been many attempts to create an updated multidimensional dashboard. The Organisation for Economic Co-operation and Development (OECD) countries, for example, have developed what they call "Wellbeing Indicators." The Kingdom of Bhutan has created a "Gross National Happiness" index, and the UN has the Sustainable Development Goals. In addition, many corporations around the world have helped develop and use the rules of the Global Reporting Initiative (GRI) for measuring their noneconomic impacts, in addition to publishing regular financial statements based on traditional accounting metrics.

Kahane (2019) emphasizes that such a paradigm shift requires immense investment; trillions of dollars per annum in impact investment. The only potential source of long-term financing is retirement programs. These can be either public sector (governmental budgets, and especially social security programs), or the pension plans, retirement and saving programs, and long-term life insurance products of the private sector.

In their paper, "Catholic Social Thought and the Economy of Communion as a Business Model," Fernández Fernández and Díaz de la Cruz (2019) investigate how Catholic Social Teaching can contribute to the creation of fairer and more humane business models. To do this, they give an outline of the main historical moments in the development of Catholic Social Teaching with regard to economics and business management. They then analyze the proposal of the Economy of Communion as a potential framework for companies that wish to implement Catholic Social Teaching in their activities.

The Economy of Communion model suggests that company profits should be distributed in three parts. The first part should be dedicated to the company's growth, development, and economic sustainability; the second towards the most needy people in the social environment of the organization (to help them overcome their situation of poverty); and the third part in the education of young people that is premised on creating a new type of economic culture that is at the service of people and of the common good.

The companies that belong to the Economy of Communion movement are for-profit businesses that consider reciprocity and gratuity an integral part of their functioning. Both reciprocity and gratuity are guided by the logic of the gift, which is innate to human relations and should be promoted so that businesses become more authentically human and favor the development of people. Fernández Fernández and Díaz de la Cruz (2019) emphasize that although the business management methods of Economy of Communion companies can be carried out by anyone, regardless of their beliefs or personal motivations, it is difficult to imagine that they will be implemented by those who do not have a genuine spiritual motivation for doing so.

In his paper, "Dignity, Love and Servant-Leadership," Hejj (2019) observes that CEOs and other top managers often think about their employees as "cost factors" to be minimized. This is not a genuine human approach. Considering other human beings as "human resources" or "human capital" means that they are used only as a means of generating financial value. There is, however, an alternative approach emerging in management theory and practice, according to which all employees are considered and treated as persons and as ends in themselves; i.e., individuals with dignity.

Hejj (2019) shows that a personalistic approach might contradict the principles of short-horizon profit maximization, but still support the long-term economic sustainability of the company—but only in the case that the latter is not just considered another "managerial tool" aimed at maximizing performance, but is rather deeply rooted in the company's DNA as part of its ethos. The fundamental principle of such an organization is implemented mutual love. Ideally, all employees and even external stakeholders will share the same value set. The key to sustaining such a culture is the leader. When top managers focus on establishing and maintaining this type of culture, they should follow a "servant-leadership" model. In his paper, Tibor Hejj proves the logic of the above-described approach and what it means in terms of day-to-day management, focusing on the leader-employee relationship.

In his paper, "Social Entrepreneurship, Conscience, and the Common Good," Chalupnicek (2019) observes that while the current body of research on social entrepreneurship contains many insights into the practical functioning of social businesses (setting-up, networking, financing, scaling, etc.), surprisingly little attention has been paid to exploring the "social" part of the concept. Questions such as "What is the most pressing social concern that should be addressed?"; "How may social business help prevent the undermining of important societal values?"; and "How can we handle conflicts of values resulting from the hybrid nature of social enterprises?" are rarely directly addressed.

Chalupnicek (2019) argues that a relational understanding of conscience, discernment, and common good can provide basic guidelines for ethical decision-making for social entrepreneurs. He challenges the widespread individualistic vision of an entrepreneur as a natural-born hero who has been called to transform society for others. On the contrary, an entrepreneur can support communication, understanding, and solidarity between social entrepreneurs and the communities in which they work. It is these relationships that can make social entrepreneurship truly social and caring.

One important illustrative example of genuine social entrepreneurship is the Mondragon Corporation, founded as a cooperative in 1956 by José María Arizmendiarrieta, a Catholic priest, in the Basque region in Spain. Today, there is a network of over 260 companies with more than 80,000 employees in fields such as finance, industry, education, and retail. Despite its size, its values still retain its original cooperative spirit: it does not define itself simply as "a business," but as "a business-based socio-economic initiative" which values—among other things—democratic organization, the subordination of capital to labor, participatory management, and wage solidarity. Mondragon challenges existing management theories by showing that cooperation and solidarity can be the basis of a successful enterprise.

In his paper, "The Caring Attitude of Christian and Buddhist Entrepreneurs," Kovacs (2019) analyzes the way a spiritual value-orientation influences entrepreneurs to develop a caring attitude in business. Kovacs presents the results of his explorative study about Christian and Buddhist entrepreneurs working in Hungary. Christian and Buddhist entrepreneurs have different ontological beliefs. Christianity is an anthropocentric tradition, while Buddhism emphasizes the intrinsic value of all sentient beings (human and nonhuman). Nevertheless, caring for others is of major relevance in both spiritual traditions. It is expressed as solidarity in the practice of Christian entrepreneurs, and as compassion in the practice of Buddhist ones.

Kovacs (2019) finds that caring appears in different but intertwined fields of business and is realized through similar business practices of Christian and Buddhist entrepreneurs. The observable shared features are as follows: (i) Such entrepreneurs take into account the interests of their employees to a great extent; (ii) They treat their stakeholders equally, as they award the same importance to suppliers and all other partners in business as they do to customers; (iii) They pay attention to preserving culture and the natural environment; (iv) They have a long-term orientation, and aim to achieve a state of long-term sustainability; (v) They define the goals of business more broadly than profit-maximization. Kovacs concludes that the main goal of spiritually based entrepreneurship is not the cultivation of material wealth, but rather the realization of human development, in which caring for others plays a major role.

In his paper, "Caring Entrepreneurship and Ecological Conscience—The Case of Patagonia Inc.," Ims (2019) argues that entrepreneurship is critical for increasing the capacity for innovation and responsiveness in business. However, not all entrepreneurial activities are geared to solving the real and most serious problems facing society. One of the biggest challenges today—Ims warns—is *climate change*, which is a major problem for Earth and, in particular, for future generations.

Ims (2019) asks what characterizes the development of the character of entrepreneurs who genuinely care about nature as a primordial stakeholder. He presents the case of Yvon Chouinard, founder of Patagonia, a clothing company that has succeeded in creating innovative solutions and has implemented a number of prosocial and proenvironmental activities that inspire other business leaders and organizations to create more sustainable practices.

Ims (2019) gives an account of the background of Chouinard's ecological consciousness that makes him and his business a role model for other companies. The paper also reflects upon what would be a fitting education for business leaders at a time when management theories and the field of economics are dominated by abstract conceptions according to which narrow self-interest and a mechanical worldview reduce nature to sets of resources.

In her paper, "Spirituality and Caring in Organizations: The Covenant Metaphor," Setter (2019) underlines the fact that *metaphors* determine the way we perceive and understand our world. There is a wide variety of metaphors for organizations, many of which depict rationality, but only a few of which express their spiritual and human side.

Setter (2019) discusses three metaphors by which the mutual entitlements and obligations of employees and organizations can be understood. The first is the transactional, market-based "balance sheet" metaphor, which is used in exchange and equity theories, where accountant-style "quid pro quo" exchanges are pertinent. The second is the legal-like "contract" metaphor, where agreements, promises, and tacit expectations about exchanges and the rules of exchange are prevalent. Finally, the spiritual metaphor of the "covenant" in the Jewish tradition is presented, by which obligations and entitlements are not dependent on other parties' fulfilling their role, and where "horizontal" relations between employees and management are complemented by "vertical" obligations to a higher cause.

Setter (2019) refers to empirical studies to show that the covenant elements are pertinent in the mutual obligations of members of business firms. Some new findings are presented in the paper that validate the idea that the employee-organization relation is partially covenantal. The chapter concludes that the covenant metaphor can be fruitfully used to describe and explain care and spirituality in organizational settings.

In his paper, "Creative Spirit in Management Education: Insights from Rabindranath Tagore," Mukherjee (2019) argues that in the wake of pervasive globalization and the triumph of capitalism and consumerism, mainstream management education has responded by churning out "products" equipped to combat aggressive competition due to demand from market forces. Business schools have become like the assembly lines of a manufacturing behemoth, where an emphasis on quantity has overshadowed the quest for quality and human excellence.

Mukherjee (2019) believes that excessive predominance of analytical, logical, and quantitatively oriented left-brain activity has led to the numbing of creative, intuitive, and holistic right-brain development. Creativity and joy in the learning experience have been sacrificed on the altar of this fossilized system just to ensure the "rigor" of pedagogical methods and processes. The victims of this mechanized and often mindless acquisition of information and utilitarian knowledge are not only students but also faculty, who are hard-pressed to manage the academic workload in the rush for promotion and tenure.

Mukherjee (2019) raises the voice of the "Other" to offer alternative sources and methods of learning in the light of valuable insights from the life and work of Rabindranath Tagore, the Nobel Laureate poet from India, who was not only a literary genius but also a musician, philosopher, artist, and a pioneer in experimenting with alternative education. He outlines the salient learning points from Tagore to enrich the presently ossified education system and bring in fresh air and new light that promotes the all-round *humanistic development* of individuals and the creation of a joyful and creative learning environment. Learning from nature, immersion in silence, and the integration of input from the humanities into mainstream management education are of extreme importance.

In his paper, "Spirituality, Caring Organizations and Corporate Effectiveness," de Bettignies (2019) states that if "spirituality" could induce entrepreneurs and leaders to build "caring organizations" that are also effective, then hope may be around the corner. But can spirituality—conspicuously absent from the core curricula of present-day management education—be taught and "developed"? If so, could business schools then begin to contribute to the building of spiritual capital and develop effective "caring" organizations? Challenging questions, but highly relevant now, particularly if business schools really desire to walk their talk: to be a "force for good."

Creating the path toward the future for the good of society—de Bettignies (2019) believes—will involve going through a tough process of questioning current management fashions and *practices*; it will require revisiting some of the "postulates" in which common management practices are rooted; it will demand intellectual curiosity that broadens the scope of our teaching to develop truly globally responsible leaders.

Learning from the benefits of the powerful medicine of spiritual practice—which has made clear the link between spiritual life and health—business schools and business leaders should together explore how to call on spirituality for the benefit of leaders, of entrepreneurs, of corporations, and of society. As violence in the streets becomes a common way of expressing dissent, we must hope that business schools will not become the scapegoats of a society that increasingly attributes the ever-more dangerous situation of our planet to their teachings.

Jonas (1984) has forcefully argued that responsibility-based caring does not presuppose any right or reciprocity. Human responsibility basically involves the non-reciprocal duty to guard beings. Responsibility implies "that of an ought-first of an ought-to–be of something, then of an ought-to–do of someone in response to the first" (Jonas, 1984: 32). This is the most evident in the case of a newborn baby "whose mere breathing uncontradictably addresses an ought to the world around" (Jonas, 1984: 32) namely, the need to take care of him or her. Not only does the newborn call us in this way, but also does "the unconditional end-in-itself of everything alive and the still-have-to-come of the faculties for securing this end" (Jonas, 1984: 32).

We care for others not because they have rights that we should respect, or because we expect something in return from them. We care for others because of *our humanity.* However, this does not mean that care is always disinterested. Caring for others, in many cases, serves our best interests. But the primary motive for caring is not self-interest, but our responsibility for the existence and well-being of others.

True humanity and genuine care are possible, even in the difficult world of business and entrepreneurship.

References

Ainsworth, M. D., Blehar, M. D., Waters, E., & Wall, S. N. (2015). *Patterns of attachment: A psychological study of the strange situation*. Psychology Press.

Bowlby, J. (1982). *Attachment and loss*. Basic books.

Bouckaert, L. (2019). Caring for being and caring for other. In O. Setter & L. Zsolnai (Eds.), *Caring management in the new economy: Socially responsible behavior through spirituality* (pp. 47–61). Palgrave-Macmillan.

Buber, M. (1937). *I and thou*. T. & T. Clark.

Bufalari, I., Aprile, T., Avenati, A., Di Russo, F., & Aglioti, S. M. (2007). Empathy for pain and touch in the human somatosensory cortex. *Cerebral Cortex*, *17*(11), 2553–2561.

Chalupnicek, P. (2019). Social entrepreneurship, conscience, and the common good. In O. Setter & L. Zsolnai (Eds.), *Caring management in the new economy: Socially responsible behavior through spirituality* (pp. 163–179). Palgrave-Macmillan.

Darwin, C. (1871). *The descent of man and selection in relation of sex* (Vol. 2nd). John Murrey Press. 403–404

de Bettignies, H.-C. (2019). Spirituality, caring organizations and corporate effectiveness: Are business schools developing such a path toward a better future? In O. Setter & L. Zsolnai (Eds.), *Caring management in the new economy: Socially responsible behavior through spirituality* (pp. 263–289). Palgrave-Macmillan.

Fernández Fernández, J. L., & Díaz de la Cruz, C. (2019). Catholic social thought and the economy of communion as a business model. In O. Setter & L. Zsolnai (Eds.),

Caring management in the new economy: Socially responsible behavior through spirituality (pp. 115–137). Palgrave-Macmillan.
Freeman, E., Harrison, J. S., Wicks, A. C., Parmar, B. L., & de Colle, S. (2010). *Stakeholder theory: The state of the art*. Cambridge University Press.
Heidegger, M. (1927). *Sein Und Zeit*. Max Niemeyer Verlag.
Hejj, T. (2019). Dignity, love and servant-leadership. In O. Setter & L. Zsolnai (Eds.), *Caring management in the new economy: Socially responsible behavior through spirituality* (pp. 139–162). Palgrave-Macmillan.
Inagaki, T., & Orehek, E. (2017). On the benefits of giving social support: When, why, and how support providers gain by caring for others. *Current Directions in Psychological Science*, *26*(2), 109–113.
Ims, K. J. (2019). Caring entrepreneurship and ecological conscience. In O. Setter & L. Zsolnai (Eds.), *Caring management in the new economy: Socially responsible behavior through spirituality* (pp. 197–220). Palgrave-Macmillan.
Jackson, K. T. (2019). Getting to the heart of compassion in philosophy and economic life. In O. Setter & L. Zsolnai (Eds.), *Caring management in the new economy: Socially responsible behavior through spirituality* (pp. 63–81). Palgrave-Macmillan.
Jacobs, G. (2019). Consciousness approach to management and economics. In O. Setter & L. Zsolnai (Eds.), *Caring management in the new economy: Socially responsible behavior through spirituality* (pp. 83–98). Palgrave-Macmillan.
Jonas, H. (1984). *The imperative of responsibility: In search of an ethics for the technological age*. The University of Chicago Press.
Kahane, Y. (2019). New Metrics for a New Economy. In O. Setter & L. Zsolnai (Eds.), *Caring management in the new economy: Socially responsible behavior through spirituality* (pp. 101–113). Palgrave-Macmillan.
Kahneman, D. (2011). *Thinking, fast and slow*. Farrar, Straus and Giroux.
Kovacs, G. (2019). The caring attitude of christian and buddhist entrepreneurs. In O. Setter & L. Zsolnai (Eds.), *Caring management in the new economy: Socially responsible behavior through spirituality* (pp. 181–196). Palgrave-Macmillan.
Levinas, E. (1961). *Totalité et infini: Essai sur l'exteriorité*. Martinus Nijhoff.
Loye, D. (2009). The ghost at the birthday party. https://www.commondreams.org/view/2009/02/12-10. Accessed December 10, 2025.
Mitroff, I. (1998). *Smart thinking for crazy times: The art of solving the right problems*. Berrett-Koehler Publishers, Inc.
Mitroff, I., & Silvers, A. (2009). *Dirty rotten strategies—how we trick ourselves and others into solving the wrong problems precisely*. Stanford University Press.
Mukherjee, S. (2019). Creative spirit in management education: Insights from rabindranath tagore. In O. Setter & L. Zsolnai (Eds.), *Caring management in the new economy: Socially responsible behavior through spirituality* (pp. 243–262). Palgrave-Macmillan.
Porter, M., & Kramer, M. (2011). Creating shared value: How to reinvent capitalism and unleash a wave of innovation and growth. *Harvard Business Review*, *89*(1–2), 63–70.
Rifkin, J. (2010). *The empathic civilization: The race to global consciousness in a world in crisis*. Polity Press.
Setter, O. (2019). Spirituality and caring in organizations: The covenant metaphor. In O. Setter & L. Zsolnai (Eds.), *Caring management in the new economy: Socially responsible behavior through spirituality* (pp. 221–239). Palgrave-Macmillan.
Ungvari-Zrinyi, I. (2019). Authentic human relations and the economy. In O. Setter & L. Zsolnai (Eds.), *Caring management in the new economy: Socially responsible behavior through spirituality* (pp. 23–46). Palgrave-Macmillan.
Yunus, M. (2011). *Building social business: The new kind of capitalism that serves humanity's most pressing needs*. Public Affairs.
Zsolnai, L. (2018). *Ethics, meaning, and market society*. Routledge.

Chapter 17
Selflessly Helping Others and the Planet

This chapter is a self-interview with the author, conducted in 2022. It discloses his spiritual path and ethical guiding principles for living and acting in a planet-positive way (Fig. 17.1).

17.1 Can You Describe Your Spiritual Path to the Buddha?

Buddhism was always attractive to me, but I started to be more interested in it when I became acquainted with E. F. Schumacher's concept of "Buddhist economics" in the early 1980s (Schumacher, 1973). The turning point came when I began studying

Fig. 17.1 Laszlo Zsolnai in 2022. *Source* Author

© The Author(s), under exclusive license to Springer Nature Switzerland AG 2026

L. Zsolnai, *Planet Positive Economy*, Springer Studies in Alternative Economics,
https://doi.org/10.1007/978-3-032-21131-6_17

the Buddhist concept of "no-self" (*anatta*) in more detail. This was revelatory for me, as it showed that a coherent and robust worldview can coexist even alongside the denial of self-centeredness.

Since my days as an economics student, I have been disgusted by the concept of self-interested action. I considered it primitive and destructive, and I still consider it so today. You cannot live like this; you can only decay like this. The modern Western worldview revolves around the realization of the "self." But the individual's—materialistically based—self-realization destroys not only the world, but also the "self." As Henrik Ibsen writes in his play *Peer Gynt*, "to be oneself—the self must die." I think this, too.

17.2 Do You Practice Buddhism?

I am not a religious Buddhist; I do not belong to any Buddhist school or sect. I wish to practice Buddhism freely, in my own way—as the great Bhutanese poet and wandering monk Drukpa Kunley (1455–1529) recommends.

I usually do simple meditation exercises, always focusing on the ethical content (*brahma-vihara*), which includes practicing "loving kindness," "compassion," "empathetic joy," and "equanimity."

17.3 How Do You Use Buddhism in Your Profession?

My field is business ethics, so Buddhist economics is an area where I can employ the ideas of Buddhism. Over the past 20 years, I have published several books, led projects, and organized international conferences in this field.

One of the first such international scientific events in the world was the conference "Economics with a Buddhist Face" that I organized in Budapest in 2007, which was attended by European, American, and Asian professors. Our next major international event was the "Contemplative Science & Management" conference in 2017, which was attended by world-renowned figures such as Clair Brown (University of California at Berkeley), Jean-Paul Jeanrenaud (University of Exeter), and Sander Tideman (Mind and Life Europe).

In my view, Buddhist economics is not a system, but a strategy that anyone can apply in any situation. The basic principle is that actions should serve to reduce the suffering of all sentient beings (human and nonhuman). So, "suffering minimization" is the main principle. The way to achieve this is through the voluntary control and reduction of human desires, the application of nonviolence (*ahimsa*), having genuine concern for the well-being of human and nonhuman others, and practicing selfless generosity. These may seem rather idealistic principles at first glance, but the results of contemporary brain research and behavioral science show their validity. There are business and social organizations around the world that operate on the basis of such principles and are able to prosper.

17.4 How Would You Summarize the Essence of Buddhism?

For me, the essence of Buddhism is liberation, not the pursuit of happiness. It is a bit misleading to sell Buddhism as the science of happiness. "Happiness" is a Western concept that does not really have an equivalent in Eastern thought. Happiness is not a goal, but a beneficial byproduct of the path to liberation. Liberation is an ethical-spiritual path. This is what the Buddha teaches, and this is what Tibetan, Zen, and other Buddhist masters teach.

17.5 What Does "No-Self" Mean in Your Interpretation?

The doctrine of no-Self means, in my opinion, that the "self" is a fiction that provides coherence and continuity in relation to an individual's existence. As the famous neuroscientist, the late Francisco Varela (1999) noted that what brain researchers find in place of the "self" is nothing more than a selfless, "virtual" self, which is a central, global pattern of the brain that is not localizable, not substantial, and functions as a virtual "interface" in the regulation of action.

The "selfless self" is one of the greatest discoveries of humanity. It gives us the opportunity to live a life that is ethereal, materially modest, but ethically and spiritually rich, instead of trying to satisfy the artificial desires of the nonexistent "self," which leads to terrible suffering for other sentient beings and to the "self" itself. A Buddhist friend of mine, the late Frans Goetghebeur, former president of the European Buddhist Union, put it this way: the task is to realize the "no-self" rather than the "self." This is a very wise thought.

17.6 What is the Main Message of Buddhism for Today's World?

The main message is that the materialistic, individualistic, self-interested way of life, which is the essence of modernity, is not a viable path. It does not lead to true well-being but may destroy the Earth. Today's ecological crisis clearly shows this. The climate catastrophe is not an "act of God," but we have brought it about, especially Western civilization with its cruel selfishness and greed. The ecological footprint of the so-called "developed" Western economies exceeds the level of sustainability by 250%–500%. If everyone wanted to live like Americans or Norwegians, then we would need three or four Earths.

Buddhism suggests that we must live differently. Frugal, that is, moderate, voluntarily restrained material consumption and selfless help to others (human and nonhuman beings) leads to liberation. Fortunately, this way of living is not only good for the Earth and other sentient beings but also good for us. Psychological and medical research confirms that reducing material desires and selflessly helping others are the key factors to achieving happiness and health. Ethics is not only good for the world, but also good for the individual.

17.7 What Can We Do in the Areas of the Economy and Social Life?

There are many things that we can do. In every area of life, there are opportunities for taking action that reduce suffering at the individual, community, and societal levels, and lead to planet positivity. I will give just a few obvious examples. Vegetarianism and veganism are such cases. If a person manages to switch to a vegetarian or vegan diet, she or he will significantly reduce the suffering of millions of animals and the enormous ecological damage caused by animal husbandry. I will never forget when my friend Peter Pruzan, a former professor at the Copenhagen Business School, said to me: "If we can live a good life without killing other beings, then why not do it?" I myself have been a vegetarian for more than 15 years, and I am also striving to achieve a vegan lifestyle.

Reducing water use, or our water footprint, is vitally important at individual, community, and societal levels. We are incredibly wasteful with water. Our irresponsible water use places a huge burden on nature and negatively impacts the lives of natural creatures. Wasting water does not make anyone happier, but other creatures suffer greatly.

Using ethical, ecological clothing and using preventive, natural medicine means a lot. Sustainable, renewable energy use, fair trade, community, and ethical banks are all relevant and important elements of the path toward planet positivity.

Of course, today's economy and society cannot be transformed overnight to function according to Buddhist principles. However, we must do what is possible. Fortunately, Buddhist action is a "game-independent" strategy, meaning that it does not require other actors to follow the same strategy in order for you to follow it. You could be the only Buddhist in the whole world and, with your actions, still help reduce the suffering of other sentient beings. In Bhutan, King Jigme Singye Wangchuck found that the animals in the country's only zoo were not happy. Therefore, he ordered that the zoo should be closed down and the animals released. There is always room for improvements. Each and every reduction or prevention of human or nonhuman suffering counts. Our job is—in the beautiful words of Hungarian poet Attila József—to "refine suffering."

17.8 What is the Relevance of Buddhism for Today's Global Society?

It is very important to demonstrate and propagate the ethos of selfless help. By setting powerful or even heroic personal examples, we can help overcome the strong materialistic value orientation of people that involves disregard for the well-being of others and the planet. Teaching altruism and practicing selfless actions should start in childhood. For example, in Budapest, in a primary school, a little girl cut off her beautiful long hair and gave it to a bald girl who had cancer so she could have a wig. This is an example of true altruism. Many such actions are needed in all areas of life.

The spread of crowdfunding models could also help a lot. It is true that "a lot goes a long way," but the most important thing is the feeling and the happiness connected with contributing to a good cause. The ethos of "creating something good" is the understanding that operationalizing the common good could be revolutionary.

However, the most important thing is to be actively involved in creating and implementing new, planet-positive working models in business, economic, and social life. Only new models can provide real hope for achieving human and ecological flourishing on Earth.

17.9 "If You Meet the Buddha on the Road, Kill Him!"—How Do You Interpret This?

Buddhism demands the complete elimination of dependence and attachment. Not only must we become independent of material possessions, but we must not become attached to any being, no matter how much we love her or him or it. This does not mean a lack of compassion. On the contrary, this "detached involvement" is the basis of genuine (nonselfish) love for others.

On the path to liberation, the Buddhist practitioner must become independent of the Buddha himself. As the great philosopher Ludwig Wittgenstein writes in his *Tractatus Logico-Philosophicus*: "My propositions are elucidatory in this way: he who understands me finally recognizes them as senseless, when he has climbed out through them, on them, over them. (He must, so to speak, throw away the ladder, after he has climbed up on it.)" (Wittgenstein, 2010: 6.54). The Buddha might have said this as well.

The goal is to create free beings in all worlds—in ourselves and others.

References

Schumacher, E. F. (1973). *Small is beautiful. Economics as if people matter*. Abacus.
Varela, F. (1999). *Ethical know-how. Action, wisdom, and cognition*. Stanford University Press.
Wittgenstein, L. (2010). *Tractatus logico-philosophicus*. Project Gutenberg. Edinburgh Press.

Index

© The Editor(s) (if applicable) and The Author(s), under exclusive license to Springer Nature Switzerland AG 2026

L. Zsolnai, *Planet Positive Economy*, Springer Studies in Alternative Economics,
https://doi.org/10.1007/978-3-032-21131-6

O

P

R

S

MIX
Papier aus verantwortungsvollen Quellen
Paper from responsible sources
FSC® C105338

If you have any concerns about our products, you can contact us on
ProductSafety@springernature.com

In case Publisher is established outside the EU, the EU authorized representative is:
Springer Nature Customer Service Center GmbH
Europaplatz 3, 69115 Heidelberg, Germany

Printed by Libri Plureos GmbH
in Hamburg, Germany